COMPLETE BOOK OF BASKETBALL'S CONTINUITY PATTERN OFFENSES

Robert Voth

Parker Publishing Company, Inc.

West Nyack, N.Y.

Library of Congress Cataloging in Publication Data

Voth, Robert
   Complete book of basketball's continuity
pattern offenses.

   Includes index.
   1. Basketball--Offense. 2. Basketball
coaching. I. Title.
GV889.V67   796.32'32   79-4297
ISBN 0-13-155937-0

Printed in the United States of America

What This Book
Will Do for You

This book gives complete and detailed access to four of the most popular and most effective offenses in basketball today: the shuffle offense, the triple stack offense, the 1-4 offense, and the passing game, also called the motion offense. These offenses have five benefits that make them both popular and effective.

First, each offense contains individual offensive moves that are extremely difficult to defense, giving you effectiveness. Second, each offense is easy to teach, saving you time to spend on other aspects of your game. Third, each offense has free-lance elements that may be used in part or in total, making your team difficult to stop or even to scout. Fourth, this book includes variations of each offense that may better suit your personnel than the original offense. They also give you a "different look." Fifth, and most important, each offense in this book is a continuity offense which can give you movement and offensive organization.

This book devotes a separate and complete chapter to each of these benefits with the exception of the last—continuity. Since each offense is a continuity offense, continuity is inherent and integral. This book deals with continuity in each step-by-step discussion of each offense.

In addition to the step-by-step explanation provided for each offense, this book includes diagrams to be used conjunctly. The most basic options are described and diagramed for each offense. Coaching hints are offered, pointing out things to look for in using each offense.

These hints give you an experiential edge over those who would learn by trial and error.

A separate chapter for each offense is devoted to drills that facilitate the teaching of each offense to your players. The drills are diagramed and use the "parts-to-whole" method of teaching.

The chapters on popular variations of each offense and the chapters on free-lance play for each offense are, in light of current defensive trends in basketball, the most important. Current defensive trends make use of pressure defenses. I prefer to call them denial defenses so as not to confuse them with pressing defenses. These denial defenses are designed and calculated to take advantage of certain faulty skills of the modern basketball player and certain tendencies of most modern basketball offenses. Concerning ourselves only with the latter for the purposes of this book, today's modern offenses tend to use two-guard fronts, initiate play with a guard-to-forward pass, overlook the importance of post play, ignore the off-side forward and guard by including only two or three men in the play at any given time, and screen for the purpose of the open shot. In addition, and in the minds of the players who must learn and use the offense, the offense becomes more important than the movement the offense was to generate or the basket that was to have been the result of the movement. These offenses are also predictable and "scoutable."

Teams who use the denial defense and who scout their opponents are able to predict what the offense will try to do and prevent them from doing it. The denial defense team plays in the passing lanes on the ball side, taking away the pass from guard to forward that starts the offense, and taking away the pass to the post, which is the heart of offensive basketball. They sag off the off-side guard and forward, an action which jams the middle and also makes it difficult to screen for the close-in, high-percentage shot. The defense has a decided advantage, and since the offense probably has only a few basic "plays" because they must be memorized, the offense may not be able to adjust until the game is already lost.

Offenses are finding that in order to be successful against the good teams today (and it is those they must defeat in order to be successful), they must be varied flexible offenses or free-lance offenses. Offensive variety must be used to counter the denial defenses. This variety must be found in variations of basic offenses such as the shuffle, in free-lance offenses whose continuity comes from rules rather than plays, or from new innovations such as the triple stack whose possibilities have just scratched the surface of its potential.

This book covers all of these contemporary offensive trends, making it, as the title suggests, the *Complete Book of Basketball's Continuity Pattern Offenses*.

Finally, this book has a subtle advantage which needs mentioning here. The offenses and their variations described in this book share many things in common. For instance, the triple stack and the 1-4 share elements of the shuffle, especially the shuffle cut. The triple stack and the 1-4 both have dynamic post play. The passing game has free-lance play which may be incorporated into other offenses discussed in this book. These offenses, systematized into a single volume, not only allow for the easy comparison of and selection from modern offensive trends in basketball, but also make it easy for you to incorporate the elements from one offense with those from another.

Robert Voth

Contents

3: Maintaining Continuity with Free-Lance Options (*continued*)

the weave to the strong side . . . Operational movement of
the weave to the weak side . . . Using the weave to enter
the ball . . . Maintaining continuity with the weave . . .
The Isolation Series: Isolating the strong-side guard . . .
Isolating the weak-side guard . . . Isolating the strong-side
forward . . . Isolating the weak-side forward . . . Splitting
the Post: Splitting the post with two players . . . Splitting
the post with three players . . . The Pick-and-Roll Series:
Picking the strong-side . . . Picking the weak-side . . .
Picking with the post . . . Picking to start the offense . . .
The Clear-Out Series: The double clear-out.

When to use the drills . . . Passing drills for the shuffle
offense . . . Drills for the cutter . . . Combining the passing and cutting drills . . . Screening drills . . . Drills for
the post . . . Rebound drills.

PART II

THE TRIPLE STACK

Advantages and disadvantages of the triple stack . . . The
basic formation . . . The secondary formation . . . Personnel requirements and placement . . . Moves that key the
offense . . . The weak-side pass . . . The strong-side pass
from the primary formation . . . Continuity for the primary
formation . . . The strong-side pass from the secondary
formation . . . Continuity for the secondary formation . . .
Rebounding the triple stack.

Advantages of the power series . . . Keying the power play
for the high post . . . Keying the power play for the low
post . . . How to beat the slougher . . . Rebounding the
power series . . . Special uses of the power series.

PART III

THE 1-4 OFFENSE

**16: Coaching the Keep-Away Game: Passing Game
for Zones** *(continued)*

formation and personnel placement . . . The basic offense
and options . . . Coaching hints for the keep-away
game . . . Cycling the keep-away game for continuity . . .
Using the keep-away game against man-to-man defense.

PART I

THE SHUFFLE

1

Coaching the Shuffle Offense

No book of basketball offenses would be complete without the shuffle offense. While the shuffle has been varied, changed, and redesigned in many different ways, it is this very variety and constant usage that attest to its importance in modern basketball. In fact, it may not be possible to catalog all of the varieties of the shuffle. However, Bruce Drake's innovation has proved to be a sound offense that could be used against all defenses or readily adapted to meet unusual defensive or offensive requirements. Aside from these obvious advantages, the shuffle offense has many more:

Advantages and Disadvantages

1. The shuffle can be used as a pattern offense or as a free-lance offense.
2. It is a well-balanced offense that uses all players.
3. It is not complicated to learn or execute.
4. Since the shuffle uses all players in all positions, it has no special player restrictions.
5. It is a team-oriented offense because all players must work and move together.
6. The shuffle forces defensive players to play away from their normally assigned positions.

The few disadvantages of the shuffle offense are:

1. Any basketball player who plays the shuffle must be a good ball handler since each player will play each position in the offense.
2. While the overall offense is easy to learn and run, it requires patience and exacting execution of minor offensive details.

Basic Formation and Personnel Placement

The exact positioning of players is really more important than which players occupy the various positions. The shuffle offense I grew up with, the one that is probably the most traditional, aligns itself as seen in Diagram 1-1. While the shuffle alignment can be set to either side of the floor, Diagram 1-1 pictures the overload on the left side, because the initial motion of the ball and the players is from left to right. This alignment presupposes natural strengths of right-handed players who prefer to pass and shoot while going to their right. Teams with left-handed players may prefer other variations.

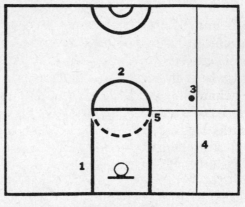

Diagram 1-1

Since the shuffle can produce a score from its initial movement, it is helpful to place players in specific positions initially. This also eliminates confusion in setting the offensive attack.

The shuffle attack begins from approximately a 2-1-2 offensive set. Unlike discussions of most 2-1-2 offenses, discussions of the shuffle do not designate players as guards, forwards or centers because in the normal operation of the offense each player will play more than one position. Here the players are simply referred to by number.

Player 1, a forward-type player, should be one step above the block-shaped hash mark at the key's edge. Player 4, the other forward type, should be higher and wider, perhaps a step outside an imaginary midpoint between the key and the sideline. He should be closer to the baseline than 5, usually the tallest player, who is next to the key and a step below the free-throw line. Player 2, the shorter of the two guard-type players, is two steps above the top of the key and in direct line with the basket. Player 3, the taller guard, is on an imaginary line dividing the area of the court between the key and the sideline into two equal parts. Once 3 is on this line he should position himself midway between 5 and 2.

I have found it useful to place the team's best ball handler in the number 1 position. Otherwise, the shuffle does not require that players have specific talents to be able to play at certain positions. If you have a player with certain limitations or a player with unusual abilities, succeeding chapters contain variations of the shuffle that may be more appropriate to your needs. These special considerations aside, standard placement of personnel is wise.

Rationale for Player Placement

The shuffle can be set to either side of the floor, and player talents and specific positions need not be matched for successful operation of the offense. Rather, I prefer the tallest guard in the 3 position because he will be going to the basket first, and his size is immediately helpful there. Player 1, who is at the forward position, can help the offense if he is a good one-on-one player, with or without the basketball, because he is in a naturally cleared out area. Playing a good post-type player at the 5 slot may be merely traditional, but I think it is also helpful to have the tall player near the basket initially. This tall player is especially helpful near the basket to rebound if 3 does attempt to score on the initial move of the offense. Positions 2 and 4 are filled by process of elimination, with the shorter guard preferred as 2.

Initiating Offensive Movement with the Shuffle Pass

The shuffle begins with passes from 3 to 2 and from 2 to 1. (Diagram 1-2) Precise attention to detail and exact execution are required for successful operation of this offense. Consequently, these initiating passes are not merely guard-to-guard and guard-to-forward.

The Guard-to-Guard Pass

Assuming that 3 brought the ball down the floor and into position for offensive initiation, 2 must anticipate when 3 will approach his normal position. At this point 2 makes a good fake-cut (perhaps only a jab-step, but often it need to be more) and returns to his spot for the pass. If 2 and 3 have coordinated their efforts, this pass can be made easily. Player 3 must know that 2's defensive player will learn to anticipate this pass and try to intercept. Player 3 must never pass to 2 if the risk of interception is too great. Rather, he should fake the pass to 2 as a signal to back-cut. This back-cut by 2 is illustrated in Diagram 1-3.

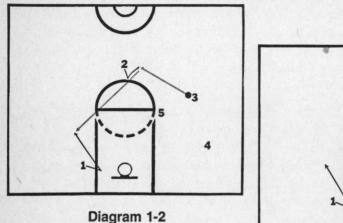

Diagram 1-2

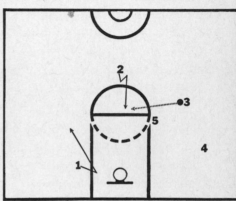

Diagram 1-3

The Guard-to Forward Pass

Player 1 uses the pass from 3 to 2, not the catch by 2, as his signal to jab-step to the basket in order to clear himself for a pass from 2. Timing is important. Player 3 will have initiated a cut to the basket in anticipation of a pass from 1. For this reason, player 1 must not delay the pass from 2.

Other Methods of Beginning

If player 2 brings the ball up the floor, he can take 3's spot on either side of the floor. If he chooses to set up on the right side, then the other players adjust accordingly. He can also initiate the offense from his 2 position at the top of the key by foregoing the pass from 2 to 3. It makes little sense to pass from 2 to 3 and back to 2 when 2 already has the ball. Player 3 times his cut to the basket so that he is in harmony with the subsequent pass from 2 to 1.

The Shuffle Cut

The cut to the basket by 3 is the shuffle cut and is the heart of the offense. Like all other portions of the offense, the shuffle cut must be well executed.

Diagram 1-4 illustrates the shuffle cut by 3. Once 3 has passed the ball to 2 he begins this cut. It is important that 3 neither fly into this move nor that he pass while actually moving to the basket. Because timing is so important, 3 should stop, pass and then begin his cut at half speed. Player 3 wants to rub his guard off on 5. Player 5 does not move to screen for 3. However, 5 makes himself as big and imposing as possible so that 3 has a good target.

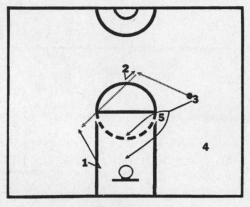

Diagram 1-4

As 3 backs his guard in toward the post, the guard must either bump into the post or go to one side or the other. When contact is made or when the guard chooses a side to slide by the post, 3 breaks away from the the guard and accelerates to full speed as he brushes shoulders with 5. This close brushing contact by 3 and 5 is important so that the guard cannot fight past 5.

Player 3 can break either way on his cut. The cut is made by planting the foot closest to the guard, shoving off from the foot into the accelerated run to the basket. Chapter 4 suggests drills for teaching this cut.

The Basic Play Pattern

To review, 3 normally initiates the offense by passing to 2 and by beginning his shuffle cut. Number 2 passes to 1. Player 1 looks to pass to 3, who has now cleared the post area. This is the initial movement of the offense and can be seen in Diagram 1-5. If 3 does not get a pass from 1, he continues through the key and becomes a forward. He will assume 4's role once the offense has reshuffled to the right side of the floor.

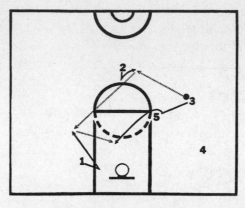

Diagram 1-5

Screening to the Strong Side

Player 2, meanwhile, hesitates for 3 to clear the post, then goes down the free-throw lane to screen for 4 and 5. Player 1 may pass to either 4 or 5. (Diagram 1-6)

If 5 doesn't get the pass from 1, then he moves to the point position vacated by 2. If 4 doesn't get the ball, then he becomes the new post on the right side of the key. Player 2 remains low, becoming the weak-side forward. His new position on the left side of the floor is similar to 1's position on the right side when the offense started.

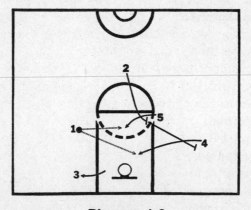

Diagram 1-6

Change of Sides Continuity

Finding no one to pass to, 1 dribbles out to initiate the reshuffled offense. (Diagram 1-7) He begins the offense's second operation by passing to 5, similar to 3's passing to 2 in Diagram 1-5. Compare Diagram 1-5 with the current action in Diagram 1-8.

Meanwhile, all players have adjusted their positions on the floor to meet the strict positioning requirements previously set down.

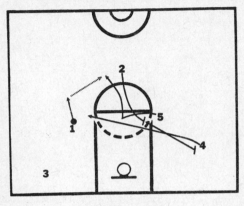

Diagram 1-7

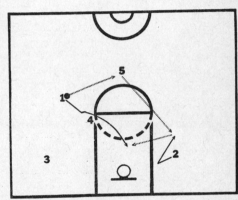

Diagram 1-8

The Shuffle's Second Cycle

Upon passing the ball to 5, 1 begins his shuffle cut. Player 5 passes to 2, who looks for 1 cutting past 4 at the post. If 1 fails to get a pass from 2, he then continues through the key to become a forward. All this movement is shown in Diagram 1-8 and is identical to the initial movement shown in Diagram 1-5 except that the offense is operating from the other side of the floor with players occupying different positions.

Diagram 1-9 shows the completion of the second shuffle. After 1 has cut past the post, 5 screens for 3 and 4; either 3 or 4 may get the ball. If neither does, then 4 moves out to the top of the key and 3 becomes the new post. The shuffle offense has now been completely run through twice.

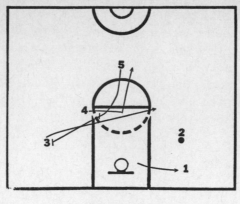

Diagram 1-9

Hidden Advantages of the Shuffle

Obviously, it will be rare that a team will have to go beyond this point for a scoring opportunity to develop. Nevertheless, for coaching purposes and for patience, coaches will insist that the offense continues to run and reshuffle to run again.

It is during the second operation of the shuffle that some of the hidden advantages of the offense become apparent. In Diagram 1-8, 1 and 5 are filling the guard positions. Now, 1 began at forward and 5 began at the post. It is assumed that their defensive players began at those positions also. These defensive players are not used to playing defense so far from the basket. Their coaches would probably prefer that they were not out there. They are not used to guards cutting to the basket.

Similarly, 2 and 3's guards are used to playing out front. Perhaps they do not position themselves well near the basket for either defense or rebounding. Because all of these defensive players are in unfamiliar positions, they will be prone to mistakes. This reasoning should be conveyed to the offensive players so that they learn to value patience and execution.

The Complete Offense

Up to this point, the offense has been traced through two complete cycles. If the offense is continued through three more complete cycles, each player will end up in his original floor position. In Diagram 1-10, player 2 has the ball; 3 is the new post with 4 at the point and 1 and 5 at the forward positions. Player 2 dribbles out to the strong guard position and passes to 4. Player 2 initiates the shuffle cut past 3 at the post while 4 is passing to 5.

If 2 does not get a pass from 5, then 4 screens down for 3 and for 1. (Diagram 1-11) Failing to get a pass, 3 moves out to the point, and 1 becomes the post. The offense has now undergone the complete third cycle.

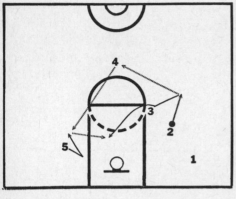

Diagram 1-10   **Diagram 1-11**

The Shuffle's Fourth Cycle

Player 5 now dribbles out to the strong guard position to begin the fourth cycle, as seen in Diagram 1-12. The shuffle pass is made from 5 to 3 to 4, and 5 shuffle-cuts past 1 at the post.

If 5 isn't open on the shuffle cut, then 3 screens for 1 and 2 as illustrated in Diagram 1-13. Should no scoring opportunities present themselves, 1 takes the point and 2 the post. The fourth cycle of the shuffle has now been completed.

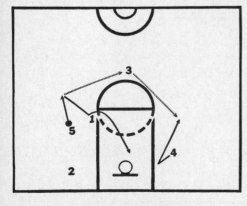

Diagram 1-12

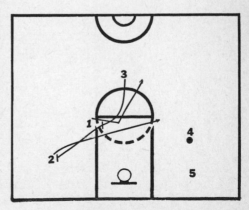

Diagram 1-13

The Shuffle's Fifth Cycle

For the fifth cycle to begin, 4 must dribble to the strong-side guard position as shown in Diagram 1-14 and pass to 1 at the point. Player 1 passes to 3 at the weak forward position as 4 shuffle-cuts past the post player, 2. Continuing with the offense, 1 goes to screen for 2 and 5 as 4 clears the key. Player 2 takes the point, his initial position. The post is once again occupied by 5; 1 resumes his weak-side forward position. Player 4 is back at the strong forward position, and 3 dribbles to his station to begin the offense in Diagram 1-15 just as he did in Diagram 1-4.

Diagram 1-16 shows the alignment of the shuffle after five complete cycles. Compare it with Diagram 1-4.

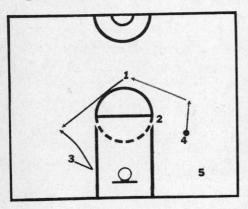

Diagram 1-14

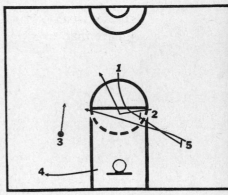

Diagram 1-15

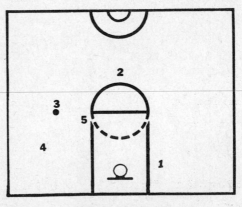

Diagram 1-16

Handling Trouble Spots in the Shuffle

Because the shuffle is so potent, defenses will try to adjust to survive. The adjustments they try to make usually come in two areas. The first of these adjustments will be to overplay the shuffle pass in hopes of stealing it. If the defense is successful in this, they have prevented the offense from even beginning. The second adjustment will be the sloughing of players into the key area to help defend against the shuffle cut, which is the heart of the offense.

Here are some coaching hints to counteract these defensive ploys and help maintain the potency of the shuffle offense.

The Back-Door Options

As indicated earlier, the shuffle pass from guard to guard to forward is more than a possible problem, because the offense begins with this pass every time and the defense learns to anticipate it. This anticipation will lead to defensive steals unless something is done to take away the threat.

Earlier in this chapter, we suggested that both the point guard, player 2, and the forward, player 1, should make earnest moves to the basket to back their defensive guards toward the basket. This little detail, when done correctly, makes it much easier to complete the shuffle pass.

Diagram 1-17 shows a typical defense against the shuffle. All of the defensive players are playing honest defense except the guard on player 2. This defensive guard is overplaying the passing lane to the

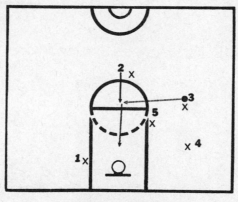

Diagram 1-17

ball in hopes of intercepting the pass from 3. If 2 makes his move to the basket and the guard doesn't respect it, then 2 will have the lay-up as pictured. If the guard respects the move, then 2 will be open as seen in Diagram 1-2.

Back-Door Plays for the Weak-Side Forward

This same back-door play is effective against defensive cheating on the weak-side forward. Diagram 1-18 illustrates 2 with the basketball; all defensive players are playing honestly except the guard on player 1. He is overplaying, hoping to steal the ball as it is passed from 2. If 1 starts for the basket and isn't followed, then he should get the pass from 2 for the ensuing lay-up. If the guard defends the back-door cut, 1 should be open coming out for the pass as seen in Diagram 1-2.

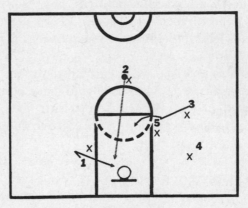

Diagram 1-18

Coaching the Shuffle Pass

To further the success of the shuffle pass, coaching proper passing technique will be helpful.

Begin by having player 3 pick up his dribble if he is unable to drive his defensive player, put the ball overhead and look into 5 at the post. This move will help freeze the guard playing defense on 2 since he may anticipate dropping back to help defend the post if the ball should go there. It should also help tighten the defense on 5, making it more difficult for 5's defensive player to switch to 3 during the shuffle cut.

Once 3 has looked inside and 2 has cleared himself by faking the back-door pass, the pass should be able to be made. The pass itself should be made from the overhead position after turning the body slightly toward 2. It should be made quickly and crisply with the wrists.

Player 2 should catch the ball, pull it overhead and pass quickly to 1. Player 2 should never hold the ball or delay the pass in any way, unless he is positive that he can beat his man on the dribble. Any delay by 2 will result in getting the ball to 1 too late for the relay to 3.

Combating the Post Switch

If the offense is consistently successful in completing the shuffle pass, the defense will begin to slough towards the middle to help defend against the shuffle cut. The first thing defenses try to do is switch their player guarding 5 at the post onto the cutter, player 3. Part of the solution to this problem is the look-in by 3 to the post mentioned in the previous section. What to do if the ball should be passed to the post will be discussed in succeeding chapters.

If the defensive guard on 5 switches to 3 on the shuffle cut, then the post must know this and roll to the basket immediately. Player 1 should get the ball to 5 since 5 will be going to the basket with a smaller defensive player on the wrong side of him. This roll to the basket is shown in Diagram 1-19.

If nothing develops, then 4 and 5 exchange places so that the offense may continue with the down screen by 2 as seen in Diagram 1-20. Player 2 now screens for 4 who has taken the post position vacated by 5; next, 2 screens for 5 in the corner.

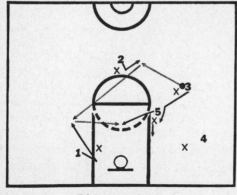

Diagram 1-19

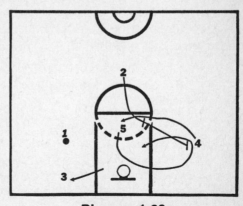

Diagram 1-20

The Strong-Side Quick Entry

en the offense successfully combats the switch at the post, the logical area from which the defense is able to get help is the player guarding 4. Since 4 is the last player to be activated by the offense and since h   always cuts to the middle, then 4's defensive guard may try to sag to the middle as shown in Diagram 1-21. Notice where 4 and 5's guards are playing. One is on each side of the post so that it will be very difficult for 3 to get free when he shuffle-cuts. Also notice how open 4 is. Simply have 3 hit 4 for the wide-open jump shot; his guard will have to move back to him and open up the middle.

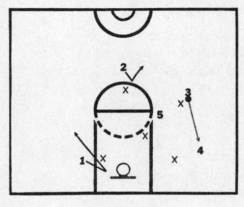

Diagram 1-21

The Forward Cross

Another move that is effective against the sagging forward is the forward cross. Notice that in Diagram 1-22 the defense sloughs off 4 to help the middle. By crossing the forward to the opposite sides of the key and posting them up, they become open targets for a pass from either 2 or 3. If the ball gets close to the basket, good one-on-one play should produce a score. Sometimes one of the forwards gets a pass in the key, on the inside of his defensive player, and a wide open shot will result.

The Post's Outside Option

Diagram 1-23 shows one final method of combating the switch at the post. If 5 is a good outside shooter (you may wish to put a good shooter there for a time if 5 is not) this option will be useful. Simply bring 2 down to screen a little sooner and look for 5 on the outside

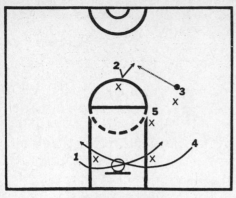

Diagram 1-22

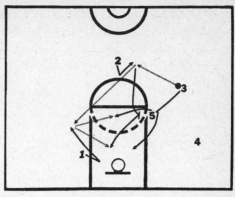

Diagram 1-23

jump shot off this screen. If 5's guard switched to cover 3, then the only players in 5's area should be the shorter players.

If 2's guard begins switching early to cover 5, then roll 2 to the basket inside his defensive player as shown in Diagram 1-23.

The Baseline Reverse

The baseline reverse by any player in the number 3 position may be the best coaching hint for the success of the shuffle. Many times, 3 will not get the ball in good scoring position. Whether it is the fault of the defense or the fault of the offense, 3 has a problem. Chances are he has overrun the lay-up area and is between the backboard and the baseline so that he cannot shoot. He will also have a guard between him and the basket.

Player 3 must know where the defense is, catch the ball, reverse-pivot to the basket, thereby locking the defense onto his back, and shoot the ball. Diagram 1-24 illustrates this.

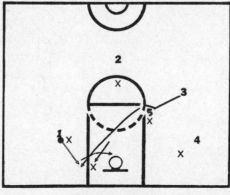

Diagram 1-24

This move is difficult for a right hander because it makes him go to his left. Many times, the shooting angle is so poor that 3 doesn't have the backboard for help. The shot can be a hook, lay-up or jump shot. All shots must be practiced with proper footwork for the pivot.

2

Developing
Popular Variations
of the Shuffle

When Bruce Drake developed the shuffle offense, it was heralded as the solution to a variety of offensive problems. It could be used effectively against all defenses. It required no special personnel to insure its success. In fact, average players who executed the shuffle well as a team defeated more talented teams who did not play together as well.

By and large, the shuffle still does these things today. That the shuffle offense still works and is still used illustrates that it has withstood the test of time. It is a great offense.

However, much has changed in basketball since the shuffle was first popularized: new rules, different styles of play, unforeseen crowd expectations, the dominance of the tall player, varied coaching philosophies, more skilled players and highly sophisticated defenses. With so many changes in the game, it is only natural that the shuffle should change as well.

Even in its many various forms the shuffle is still a great offense. In fact, it is a great tribute to its usefulness that the shuffle can be so readily adapted.

This chapter embraces a few of these evolutionary forms of the shuffle. Each may be used as a complete offense, to complement the original shuffle offense, or may be combined with other offenses contained in this book, affording you a basis for the completion of your own offensive thinking.

Why Variations Were Devised and What They Do

Included here are three evolutions of the shuffle: the tandem shuffle, the back-door shuffle and two varieties of the big-man shuffle. Each variety is different because they were designed to meet and solve different problems.

The tandem shuffle was designed to combat sloughing defenses. It is a potent offense that can run from a single stack alignment. The tandem is placed near the basket to constrict the defense. Its pattern is altered slightly from the original shuffle, but it brings great confusion to the defense. It can easily be altered further than it is in its presentation here.

Moreover, it is a shooters' offense, even if the offense has only one good shooter; this makes it an explosive, exciting offense to coach.

By varying it slightly, the tandem can become the simplified shuffle that Carroll L. Williams described in a book by the same name, a 1971 Parker publication.

The tandem shuffle also blends nicely with the triple stack attack described in Part II of this book and with the high-post passing game contained in Part IV.

The back-door shuffle is the shuffle's answer to modern pressure defense. It exploits the weak-side "zoning" characteristic of modern pressure defenses.

The back-door shuffle can be used to implement the effective, contemporary European technique of screening on the strong side of the floor and then passing to the weak side instead of passing to the screener rolling to the basket.

It can be used as a pattern offense or a free-lance offense. It is similar in some respects to and can be used in conjunction with the 1-4 offense described later in this book.

The big-man shuffle is a logical evolution of the offense for the team that is blessed with the very tall center. This offense keeps the center in the post area around the key without disturbing the shuffle's famous continuity and movement. It will blend well with forms of the passing game as well.

The Tandem Shuffle

The tandem shuffle offers many possibilities offensively, each of which is a source of consternation for the defense. I genuinely believe that it can be used with any style of play.

Advantages of the Tandem Shuffle

1. The tandem can be used to keep the tall players near the basket.
2. The tandem can be used to free the good jump shooter.
3. The tandem isolates two players near the basket for two-on-two basketball, thereby eliminating any defensive help.
4. The tandem utilizes the shuffle cut.
5. It can be used as a quick-hitting offense or as a ball control offense.
6. It forms the basis for pattern play, but can be used for free-lance play as well.
7. It is easy to learn and fun to run.
8. The tandem is a good offense for teaching individual fundamentals and team play at the same time.
9. It can be run to either side of the floor to provide a different offensive look.

The Basic Formation

Diagram 2-1 depicts the basic alignment of the tandem shuffle. While this diagram shows the shuffle with its tandem overload on the left side of the floor, it can be set to either side with good results. It is pictured to the left side here because most coaches will want to begin it on the left side so that teams with right-handed players can have their players cutting to the left when going to the basket. This enables right handers to pass and shoot from their left foot and keep the ball in their right hand, away from the defense.

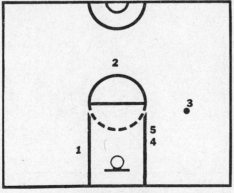

Diagram 2-1

Player 2 is at the top of the key. Player 1 is a step outside of the free-throw lane and a step above the block-shaped hash mark at the key's edge. Place player 3 at the free-throw line extended or slightly lower and midway between the free-throw lane and the sideline.

Player 5 is at the left side of the lane (as you face the basket) and midway between the backboard and the free-throw line; 4 is three feet directly behind him. Both 4 and 5 should be far enough outside the free-throw lane to prevent them from accidentally stepping into the key area and violating the 3-second rule.

Personnel Considerations

Two of the outside players, 3 and 1, should be good ball handlers. They need to be able to pass the ball well, and it is helpful if they are good drivers.

The tallest guard should be number 3. Player 2 should be the shorter guard, and 1 is the short forward.

Player 5, the post player, is usually the tallest. His position does not require special talent. In fact, this position is a good one in which to use the least agile player effectively. The number 4 position can be used by either the tall forward, a second post or a good jump shooter. This choice of players at the number 4 spot will be determined by the style of play that you decide to use. The style of play can be easily changed by changing players at the number 4 position.

The Basic Offensive Pattern

Diagram 2-2 shows the initiation of the offense. Player 3 has the ball and shuffle-passes to 2 who has cleared himself by faking to the basket. Player 3 now begins his shuffle cut. After catching the ball, 2

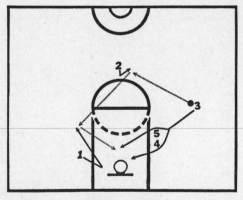

Diagram 2-2

shuffle-passes to 1 who has also cleared himself. The clearing motion, the shuffle pass and the shuffle cut are each described in the first chapter's description of the basic shuffle.

Player 3 has the option of either going over the top of the double screen set by 4 and 5 or going behind it. The double screen is an obvious advantage for the shuffle cut because of the wider screening area it affords. It should be easy for 3 to lose his guard. If either 4 or 5's defensive players switch to cover 3, then that unguarded player should roll to the basket.

If no switch occurs, then 4 cuts around 5 and into the key for the scoring pass from 1. (Diagram 2-3) If 4 is unable to get a pass, he posts up, 3 moves up behind him and 5 adjusts his position on the other side of the floor. This is shown in Diagram 2-4.

Diagram 2-3   **Diagram 2-4**

The Tandem Shuffle's Continuity

Player 1 now shuffle-passes to 2 who shuffle-passes to 5. The shuffle cut is made by 1. Player 3 follows around 4 at the post. (Diagram 2-5)

Diagram 2-6 shows that if no scoring opportunities occur, then 3

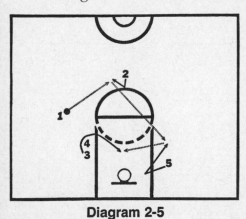
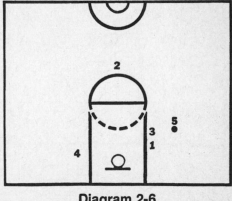

Diagram 2-5   **Diagram 2-6**

posts up with 1 behind him. Player 5 will now shuffle-pass and shuffle-cut, and the offense will run through again, maintaining the play's continuity.

The Point Guard

You will notice that 2 has become a stationary ball player. This is a disadvantage of the offense, unless 2 is the type of player who is good defensively and not up to par offensively. If this is the case, then the offense works to advantage. Player 2 can contribute defensively and maintain defensive balance for the team while on offense. If the team using the tandem shuffle is a ball-control team, 2's defensive guard will relax on defense and soon become susceptible to a back-door cut by 2.

Free-Lance Moves in the Tandem Shuffle

One of the real advantages of the tandem shuffle is the explosiveness and power generated by its free-lance moves.

For example, Diagram 2-7 illustrates the quick jumper afforded 4 as he steps up to receive a pass from 3, turns and shoots over the screen of 5 who is stationary. If 4 is a good shooter, this play can be devastating because it is very difficult to defend man-to-man. Also, notice that as 4 shoots, both 1 and 5 are in good rebound position.

Similarly, Diagram 2-8 shows 5 receiving a pass at the post and turning to shoot over 4. This move is equally difficult to defend. The shooting angle of 5 is not as good as that of 4 in Diagram 2-7, however.

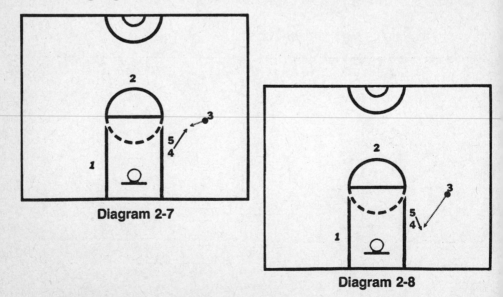

Diagram 2-7

Diagram 2-8

Consider Diagram 2-9. Here, 4 comes out a bit farther to get the ball from 3. His defensive guard comes, too, in a hurry to stop the anticipated jump shot. Notice where this leaves 5's defensive player. If 5 is taught good basic post play and how to maintain position, he should be able to go to the basket with the pass from 4.

Diagram 2-10 shows the same play except that 5's guard left him to switch over the top and stop the shot by 4. The difference here is that the remaining defensive player is trapped on the baseline behind 5, leaving 5 open for the short hook or jump shot.

The two-on-two post play seen in Diagrams 2-9 and 2-10 is equally effective if 5 steps out for the pass, as previously seen in Diagram 2-8. In fact, it is a nice variation to help keep the defense honest.

Finally, think of the defensive problems caused by the unusual splitting of the post seen in Diagram 2-11. Given time, the defense will learn to zone this play. If used sparingly, however, 2 will be open behind the double screen for a good shot with a great backboard angle.

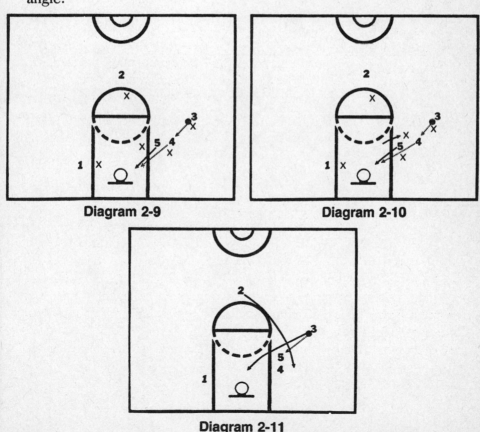

Diagram 2-9   Diagram 2-10

Diagram 2-11

The Back-Door Shuffle

Modern pressure defense pits intense overplay on the ball and players on the ball-side of the floor while the defensive players on the weak side of the floor sag and zone. If there is no offensive movement to counteract the weak-side zoning, then three offensive players must play against five defenders.

The back-door shuffle is a good offense to combat pressure defense. It minimizes ball handling on the side with the defensive overplay on the weak side of the floor, exploiting the defensive sag.

Uses of the Back-Door Shuffle

As indicated above, the back-door shuffle is a good offense to use against pressure defense. It has continuity so that it can be rerun again and again. Since most teams cannot maintain good defensive posture beyond three offensive thrusts, so long as the ball changes sides of the floor each time, the continuity is an important part of beating the pressure defenses.

The back-door shuffle is also very effective against the sagging of the defensive post or the defensive weak-side forward. It is effective because it clears out the baseline area, thereby making it difficult to sag these defensive people to help defend the shuffle cut.

The back-door shuffle is also effective against match-up zones. It clears out the baseline area and then cuts a guard through the key. The defensive player on the offensive guard must either let him go unguarded or abandon the match-up zone to cover; either works to the offense's advantage.

The Basic Formation

As illustrated in Diagram 2-12, the back-door shuffle operates from a formation nearly identical to that described in Chapter 1. The only difference is that player 4 is slightly lower and slightly wider than he would be in the traditional shuffle alignment. This alignment is an obvious advantage to a team that runs the regular shuffle, since two offenses can be run from the same formation.

Likewise, the movement of the offense is an advantage to the team that runs the 1-4 offense because it uses the 1-4 configuration at one phase of the offense.

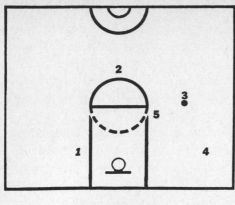

Diagram 2-12

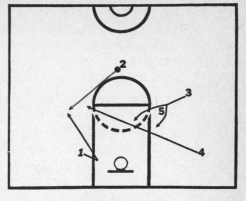

Diagram 2-13

Personnel Considerations

Traditional placement of players in the offense works well. Guards occupy the 2 and 3 positions, with 3 being the taller. The tall forward is the number 4 player, and 1 is the other forward. Player 5 is the tallest player on the team.

It is helpful if both guards in this offense are rather tall since they both go to the baseline and must often rebound from there. It is further helpful if 4 is nearly as tall as 5 since they must both play the post positions. However, size lends advantage only; it is not necessary for the success of the offense.

Operational Movement of the Offense

Diagram 2-13 illustrates the beginning of the back-door shuffle. Player 2 has the ball instead of 3, who would have it in the traditional shuffle. The reason for beginning the offense at 2 is to get the ball to the point without having to pass it there. Pressure defense does not want the ball to change sides of the floor. Nor does pressure defense desire the ball in the center of the floor; when it is there, no strong side has been declared to overplay, and no weak side (or help side) has been established to sag from.

As 2 approaches his area, a step or two from the top of the key, 1 jab-steps toward the basket to clear himself. At the same time, 4 explodes across the key to a post position similar to that of 5. If 4 is open in the key enroute to his new position, he should get the ball for the try at the basket. If he is not open, it will be because his guard, who will probably be sagging toward the key, picked him up. This is a good thing because it reduces the amount of weak-side help that the defense can muster.

The alignment is now roughly that of the 1-4. Player 2 can pass to 1, 4, 5 or 3. From the time that the ball is passed, the offense will be the same, regardless of who gets the pass.

It is preferred that 1 get the pass since this is the way that the shuffle would run. This would take advantage of the tall guard, 3, going to the basket. It also means that the first scoring movement would be from right to left. However, this is not critical. Diagram 2-12 shows either 1 or 4 getting the ball.

Diagram 2-13 shows that 1 gets the pass as 3 shuffle-cuts to either side of 5. He continues through the key if he fails to get the ball. The pass can come from 4 as well as from 1. Diagram 2-14 shows that the left side of the floor cleared out because of 3's shuffle cut. Player 2 now cuts back-door off 5 instead of screening from him as in the traditional shuffle. Player 5 can roll to the basket as seen in Diagram 2-14.

If 5 doesn't roll or doesn't get the pass, he moves out to the point to receive the shuffle pass from 1. This initiates the back-door shuffle again, this time from the right side of the floor. See Diagram 2-15.

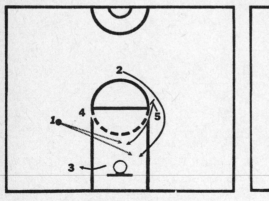

Diagram 2-14

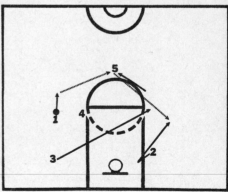

Diagram 2-15

The Big-Man Shuffle

Occasionally a team employing the shuffle offense will be blessed with a very tall player. These teams may prefer keeping this player close to the basket while still running the shuffle. The big-man shuffle keeps the post player, number 5, near the basket. The big-man shuffle involves four players in the pattern and rolls the post player from side to side, thereby keeping him near the basket.

The Basic Formation and Personnel Placement

The basic formation of the big-man shuffle offense is the same as that of the traditional shuffle outlined in Chapter 1. Diagram 2-16 illustrates the player alignment for the big-man shuffle. Players 2 and 3 are the guards, the taller being 3; 1 and 4 are the forwards with 4 being the taller. The tall player occupies the post position indicated by 5 in the diagram.

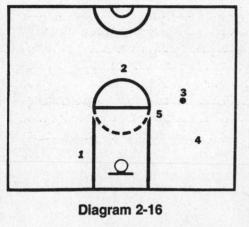

Diagram 2-16

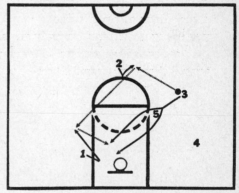

Diagram 2-17

The Operation of the Big-Man Shuffle

Like the traditional shuffle offense, the big-man shuffle begins with the shuffle pass from 3 to 2 to 1. This is illustrated in Diagram 2-17 along with the traditional shuffle cut by 3 after he has passed the ball to 2. If 3 should be open while cutting to the basket, then 1 should pass the ball to 3 for the score.

If the guard defending 5 should switch to cover 3 as seen in Diagram 2-18, then 5 should roll to the basket.

If the defensive player guarding 5 did not switch, 5 should make a quick move to the ball, either over the top of the defense or behind it. Diagram 2-19 illustrates.

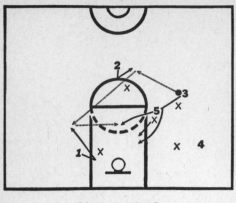

Diagram 2-18   **Diagram 2-19**

Should 1 have been unable to get the ball to 3 or 5, both players assume new positions on the opposite side of the floor. Player 3 becomes the strong-side forward and 5 again becomes the post. Since 1 has the ball near 3 and 5 on the strong side, the strong-side entry discussed in Chapter 1 may be employed at this point.

Meanwhile, 2 and 4 interchange on the back side of the offense. Player 2 may be open on his move to screen for 4, and 4 may be open cutting off 2's screen. At any rate, they interchange to complete the offensive movement.

The Big-Man Shuffle's Continuity

The big-man shuffle gets its continuity when 1 dribbles out to the strong-side guard position, passes to 4 (who passes to 2) and shuffle-cuts off 5 at the post. See Diagram 2-20. The post player, 5, now moves into the key for a pass from 2 and then takes up a position on the other side of the key.

Diagram 2-21 illustrates the completion of the second "change of sides" continuity of the big-man shuffle as 4 screens down for 2 and they interchange on the back side.

The Shuffle for Two Big Men

Should a team be blessed with two tall players and wish to keep both near the basket, this variation of the shuffle can accomplish that goal.

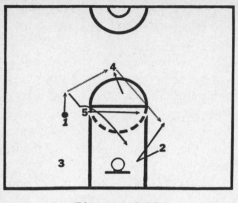

Diagram 2-20

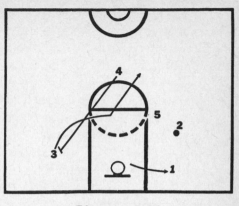

Diagram 2-21

Basic Formation and Personnel Placement

The illustration seen in Diagram 2-22 is the formation for the shuffle for two tall players. From Diagram 2-22 it is easily seen that the formation for this offense is nearly identical to that of the traditional shuffle of Chapter 1. If any change could be noted, it would be that 4 is slightly closer to the basket than in the traditional shuffle.

The two tall players occupy the 4 and 5 positions. They maintain these positions on one side of the floor or the other throughout the operation of the offense. The three smaller players interchange, but their initial alignment seen in Diagram 2-22 should have the short forward in the 1 position and the tall guard in the 3 position.

Diagram 2-22

Operation of the Offense

Diagram 2-23 depicts the now familiar shuffle pass around the horn from 3 to 2 to 1 and the subsequent shuffle cut by 3. The offense begins to take on a new look in Diagram 2-24, however. Player 3, who didn't get the ball while cutting to the basket, swings wide outside to the point position instead of stopping at the baseline.

Following the shuffle cut, 5 makes the quick roll to the ball and posts-up on the opposite side of the floor as he did in the shuffle for one big man. Player 2 screens down for the tall player at 4, but does not interchange with him. Player 4 cuts across the key to the ball and takes up a position identical to the one he held on the other side of the floor. Player 2 rolls outside expecting the pass around the horn to initiate the continuation of the offense.

Notice 3 at the top of the key. The left side of the floor has been cleared out for him to cut to the basket or come back to the pass from 1 as seen in Diagram 2-24.

Diagram 2-23

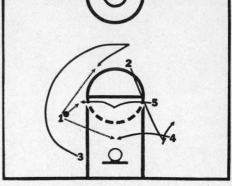

Diagram 2-24

Continuity

Diagram 2-25 illustrates the beginning of the continuity with the shuffle pass from 1 to 3 to 2. The shuffle cut is now made by 1, and 5 rolls to the ball.

Diagram 2-26 illustrates the continuity further, showing the down-screen and roll by 3, the cut by 4 off the screen of 3 and the swing to the point by 1.

This concludes the pattern variations of the shuffle offense. In the next chapter, free-lance options will be presented to further augment the basic shuffle.

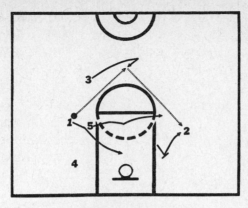

Diagram 2-25

Diagram 2-26

3

Maintaining
Continuity with
Free-Lance Options

As indicated in Chapter 2, the shuffle offense may not be completely effective by itself. The defense will learn to anticipate the basic, repetitive movement of the shuffle and cheat to defend it. The defense will sag and slough in some areas and overplay in others.

Defensive cheating can and should be exploited. To fail to do so could be a great disadvantage to the offense. The solution to defensive cheating is simple—vary the offense.

Some variations of the shuffle offense were detailed in Chapter 2. Another kind of variation, however, is the play that can occur out of the shuffle's offensive alignment. The free-lance play utilizes one-on-one, two-on-two, and three-on-three opportunities.

This chapter is entitled "Maintaining Continuity with Free-Lance Options." The title may seem paradoxical since continuity implies pattern offense and free-lance implies the lack of pattern. However, many free-lance offenses have continuity to sustain their offensive movement. So the term free-lance doesn't necessarily mean loss of continuity.

Also, defensive cheating can force teams out of their offensive pattern, which will result in a loss of continuity. So the term "continuity offense" doesn't guarantee continuity.

By using simple free-lance options to keep the defense honest, the continuity of the shuffle can be preserved. In fact, the shuffle itself is made more potent because the defense cannot anticipate and cheat against it.

How to Decide Which Options to Use

The free-lance options of the shuffle will complement the shuffle, any of its variations and many other offenses or variations of offenses described herein. Deciding which free-lance options to use will, of course, be up to you. You must evaluate your players' talents and the defensive problems your teams encounter.

When describing the free-lance options for the shuffle offense, the functions of each will be included for helpful analysis and evaluation.

The Weave Series

The old weave or snowplow free-lance offense provides a functional option to the shuffle. It can be operated from the shuffle's offensive set, it can be run to either side of the floor, it provides good opportunities for post play and it blends well with the shuffle.

The weave is generally used against defenses that sag and slough to the middle. Perhaps the offense doesn't like the long-range shooting options over the top of the sagging defense. If not, the weave presents a good means whereby the ball can be moved closer to the basket by constricting the defense.

Basic Formation and Personnel Placement

The weave series operates from any shuffle set except that of the tandem shuffle. It requires that three or four of the players be good dribblers, and it will require a bit of practice for the offense to learn to read defensive reactions to the weave.

Generally, the best ball handlers should be placed in the positions indicated by 2, 3 and 4 in Diagram 3-1. The fourth ball handler, if the team has one, should be at the 1 position, and the tallest player or the weakest ball handler will be at the 5 spot.

Operational Movement of the Weave to the Strong Side

Diagram 3-1 illustrates the basic shuffle alignment with the ball at 3. Instead of shuffle-passing to 2, player 3 drives the ball to the inside of 4. If he has beaten his defensive player, he should continue to the basket. If not, then he comes to a two-footed jump-stop alongside of 4 and hands the ball off to 4, who then drives the ball to the inside of 2. When he approaches 2, 4 jump-stops and hands the ball off to 2, who now drives it to the inside of 3. Meanwhile, 5 at the post position may go away to screen for 1 as seen in Diagram 3-1 or make the power slide to the basket as seen in Diagram 3-2. Anytime that 5 or 1 manages to get open, those on the perimeter should get the ball to him.

Coaches who are familiar with the weave know that a number of other options will occur besides the potent post play. The post play is potent, because as the ball is dribbled along the perimeter, the player defending the post will find himself on the wrong side of the post. The other options occur, however, when the ball is driven to the inside of an adjacent player.

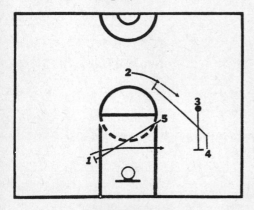

Diagram 3-1   **Diagram 3-2**

For instance, in Diagram 3-3 when 3 drives the ball to the inside of 4 for the hand-off, two things happen immediately. The ball has moved the defense so that they dare not sag, and the handoff forces the defense to switch or allow 4 to drive over the top of the screen as in Diagram 3-3.

If the defense switches, then 3 can roll to the basket as in Diagram 3-4. Or, if the switch is merely an exchange of players and done rather loosely, then 3 can abort the handoff, crossover-dribble and drive to the basket as in Diagram 3-5.

Diagram 3-6 shows that 3 dribbled to the inside of 4, jump-stopped and reverse-pivoted on his inside foot so as to screen 4's defensive player. Player 4 now cuts along the baseline for the lay-up.

Finally, if the ball is within four feet of the key, I would recommend that 3 abandon the handoff and execute the move to the basket made legal by Rule 4, Section 25, Item 3. This move is not illustrated here, but it is executed by jump-stopping on both feet, taking a cross-over step to the basket with the outside foot and laying the ball in.

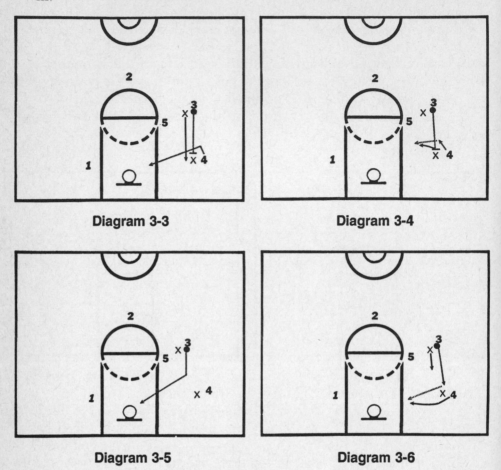

Diagram 3-3   Diagram 3-4

Diagram 3-5   Diagram 3-6

This weave can be run several times to the left side until the defense falters or until the offense has moved near enough to the basket that they feel comfortable taking a shot or abandon the weave in favor of the shuffle. Converting the weave into the shuffle is a technique that will be explained later in the chapter.

Operational Movement of the Weave to the Weak Side

Diagram 3-7 illustrates the weave being run to the right side. The weave to this side is initiated by 2 from the point. Player 2 drives the ball to the inside of 1, jump-stops and hands the ball to 1. Player 1 now drives to the inside of 3, jump-stops and hands him the ball, whereupon 3 continues the weave. All of the options accompanying the weave can be used to take advantage of the defense. Meanwhile, 4 and 5 are interchanging, either by screening away from the ball as in Diagram 3-7 or by means of the post power move.

Using the Weave to Enter the Ball

Diagram 3-8 illustrates how the weave can enhance the shuffle offense. Player 3 drives the ball over the top of 5. At the instant that 2 cuts past 3, 3 has the option to hand the ball to 2, to weave to 4 or hit 1 as seen in Diagram 3-8.

Diagram 3-7

Diagram 3-8

By hitting 1 with the pass, the shuffle has been started and 2 and 3 merely exchange roles. Player 2 has the advantage, however, of a double screen on his pseudo-shuffle cut. Player 3 screens down for 5 and 4 to maintain the continuity of the shuffle.

This move is also excellent against pressure on the guards. If the shuffle pass from 3 to 2 cannot be made because of defensive pressure, then this is a good method of beginning the shuffle. Also, if 3 started to drive to the right side and gave it up, the shuffle could be run from that point without having to reset the offense.

Diagram 3-8 illustrates how the weave option and the shuffle complement each other.

Maintaining Continuity with the Weave

If the defense cheats, as by sloughing, the weave can be used to force the defense back into an honest alignment. Once this is done, the weave can be continued or abandoned in favor of the shuffle as in Diagram 3-8. The defense, since it is forced into an honest alignment, is now vulnerable to the regular shuffle once more.

Diagram 3-9 illustrates the shuffle being started from the weave in a different fashion, but similar to that of Diagram 3-8.

In Diagram 3-9, 3 began the weave to the inside of 4. Player 4 took the ball and drove to the inside of 2 at the top of the key. Instead of handing the ball off to 2, 4 passes to 1 to begin the shuffle. Player 2 cuts back-door on the pseudo-shuffle cut, and 4 screens down for 5 and 3 to maintain the continuity.

Diagram 3-10 shows the maintenance of continuity from the weave to the weak side. Player 2 begins the weave by driving at the inside of 1. Player 3 beats his defensive player on the shuffle cut. Since the ball is at the weak-side forward position, it is in position to pass to 3 as he cuts. Player 1, who did not get the weave handoff, continued to the top of the key to screen down for 5 and 4.

Inventive coaches may find other ways to blend the weave and the shuffle together. For instance, the four-man weave can be used to involve all of the players except the post. The post can be used effectively by breaking from side to side, always toward the ball.

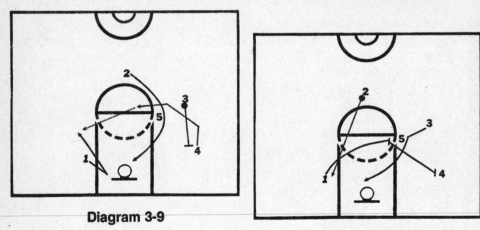

Diagram 3-9

Diagram 3-10

The Isolation Series

While the weave series for the shuffle is optional, the isolation series is believed by some coaches to be almost indispensable to the successful operation of the shuffle.

The isolation series is a series of individual moves that react to defensive cheating. They are very basic and, if keyed by the rules, are easy to learn. By learning to watch for the application of the rules, the offensive players learn to read and react to the defense.

Isolating the Strong-Side Guard

Diagram 3-11 shows the strong-side guard being isolated. This should occur when 3's defensive man waits behind 5 for 3 to make his shuffle cut. Successful shuffle-cutting has taught this defensive player to leave early to avoid being brushed off by 5. Players 3 and 4 both watch for this, and as soon as 3's defensive player leaves early they both yell, "Cheater!" and react as follows: Player 4 comes up to screen alongside 5 while 3 steps behind the double screen. Player 2 gets the cue from the yell and ships the ball back to the waiting 3. Player 3 is now isolated behind the double screen for the open shot.

Isolating the Weak-Side Guard

Player 3, who must begin the shuffle with a pass to 2, must always watch for defensive overplay by a player who would try to steal the pass. Player 1 also tries to watch for this. As soon as 1 sees 2 being overplayed, he breaks to the foul line. Player 3 passes to 1 at the foul line, and 2 goes to the basket, rubbing off his defense onto 1. This action is depicted in Diagram 3-12.

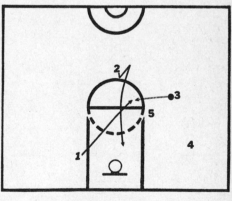

Diagram 3-12

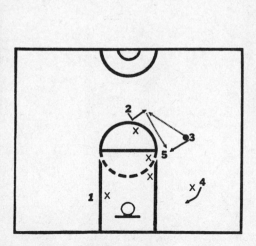

Diagram 3-11

Isolating the Strong-Side Forward

Another trouble spot in the shuffle is the sagging of the defensive player guarding 4. Sometimes this defensive player will sag as far away as the edge of the key as seen in Diagram 3-13. This will cause 3 problems when he cuts to get open, and he will have no difficulty in spotting it. Seeing such an alignment, 3 starts his shuffle cut. When he gets near 5, he yells, "Four!" and he and 5 drop down to pin the cheating defensive player into the key. Their yell alerted 2 to pass the ball to 4 behind the double screen.

Isolating the Weak-Side Forward

Diagram 3-14 shows 2 screening down for 1 to start the offense. He does this anytime he sees that 1 is being overplayed.

This move is also useful when 2 has trouble getting himself open for the pass from 3. Refer back to Diagram 1-17. Remember that 2 must make a move to the basket to get open by making his defensive player back away. If the defense does not respect this move, then 2 cuts to the basket. If 2 can't get away from a pesky defensive player or if 3 can't get him the ball by the time that 2 crosses the foul line, then 2 continues on to screen for 1 who should have no trouble getting the shuffle pass from 3.

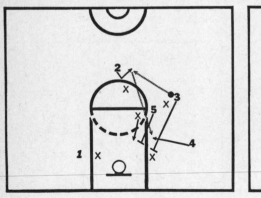

Diagram 3-13

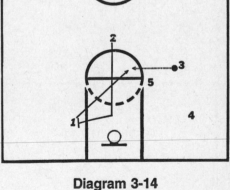

Diagram 3-14

Splitting the Post

A series of options that works well with all variations of the shuffle is splitting the post. The reason that it works so well is that the post is always open for the pass from the outside. He is open because his defensive player usually plays behind him to help defend the shuffle cut. Because of this, splitting the post becomes necessary to the operation of the shuffle.

Splitting the Post with Two Players

Diagram 3-15 shows the most common method to split the post. Player 3 usually has the ball to initiate the offense and will see that the post is open. Player 3 simply passes to the post and then splits with 2. Players 1 and 4 rotate out to preserve continuity and defensive posture.

If player 2 should begin the offense, he has the option of hitting the post and splitting it with 3 as in Diagram 3-16.

Player 3 also has the option of splitting the post with 4. This is a particularly good move if 3 has passed to 4 for a strong-side entry to the offense and 4 passed to the post as seen in Diagram 3-17.

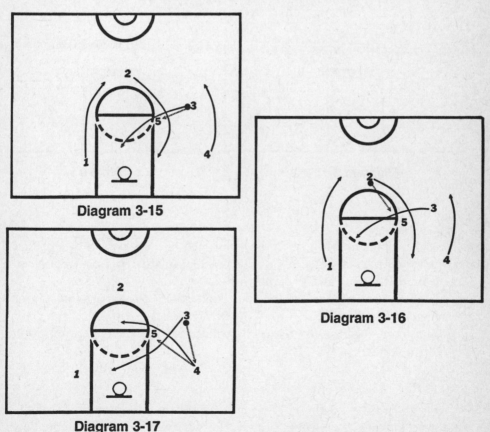

Diagram 3-15

Diagram 3-16

Diagram 3-17

Splitting the Post with Three Players

Because of the alignment of players 2, 3 and 4 in the shuffle offense, the three-player split may be triggered at any time. While it may be started in different ways, it always involves either 2 or 4 screening the other.

For instance, in Diagram 3-18 player 3 hits the post and splits. Since he breaks over the top on 2's side, 2 starts to split but continues to screen for 4 who has the advantage of a double screen enroute to the foul line. Had player 3 gone under 5, then 4 would have gone over the top to screen for 2.

If either 2 or 4 initiate the split, then the initiator screens for the other and player 3 goes opposite the screen. This can be seen in Diagram 3-19 with player 4 triggering the play.

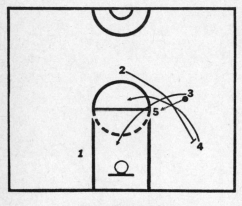

Diagram 3-18

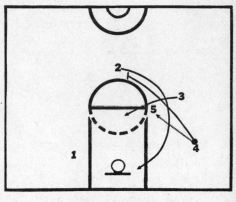

Diagram 3-19

The Pick-and-Roll Series

The pick-and-roll series is very much like the weave except that the dribbler goes outside his adjacent teammate. This difference can be used to key it as a separate series.

The pick-and-roll series is a good series to run against either sagging or aggressive defenses. Against the sag, it produces the good jump shot. Against the aggressive defenses it provides penetration with the roller.

Picking the Strong Side

Diagram 3-20 shows the pick-and-roll to the strong side of the floor. Picking the strong side works very well if 4 is playing low toward the baseline and if he waits for 3 so that the screen occurs very low. When properly executed, 3 may use the screen for the jump shot or take one more dribble to the baseline and actually lean out of bounds to pass to 4 rolling down the baseline to the basket.

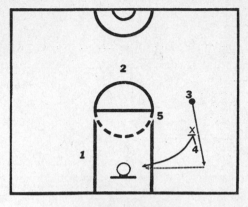

Diagram 3-20

A nice variation of this play occurs when 3 passes the ball to 4 and then cuts outside for the handoff and possible shot or drive to the basket while 4 rolls. This is seen in Diagram 3-21. Diagram 3-22 shows that 4 has the option to fake the handoff and wheel inside to the basket. This move works effectively against teams that switch very well.

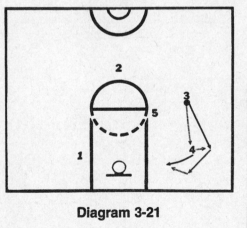

Diagram 3-21

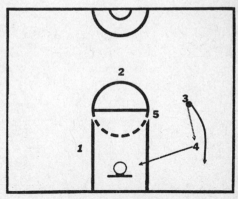

Diagram 3-22

Picking the Weak Side

Diagrams 3-23, 3-24, and 3-25 show the same pick-and-roll plays to the weak side. The basic difference from the strong-side pick-and-roll is that the pick-and-roll to the weak side need not be so near the baseline to be successful. The reason for this is that there is no post on that side.

Diagram 3-23 shows 1 coming up to screen for 2 and then rolling to the basket. This is a nice play because the shooting, passing and rolling angles are all very good.

Diagrams 3-24 and 3-25 illustrate the plays with the handoff option to the weak side.

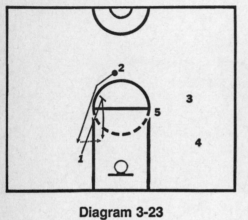

Diagram 3-23

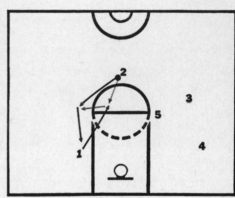

Diagram 3-24

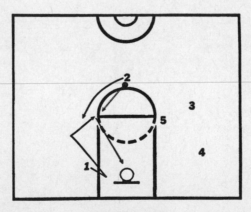

Diagram 3-25

Picking with the Post

Because the post player, 5, is usually the tallest, picking with him works well. Because he is tall he is a good target on the roll. He may pick for any of the other players by simply stepping to them, screening and rolling to the basket.

The pick-and-roll by the post can be run at any time, and because of the shuffling of players during the operation of the shuffle, other players will find themselves at the post. Once there, they will find that they can run the pick-and-roll with a good probability that the defensive players guarding them may not be used to defense post play.

The best success with the pick-and-roll by the post occurs when the post screens for 3 or 4. The defensive guard on 3 who has been sagging will not have time to recover if 3 drives him in the early screen set by 5 as seen in Diagram 3-26. A good screen here will force 5's guard to switch to 3, leaving 5 open to roll to the basket.

Recalling the strong-side entry in Chapter 1, Diagram 1-21, where 3 passes the ball to 4 with 5 sliding down the lane on a power move to the basket, we now find that 5 has the option of screening for 4 if he was unable to get the ball himself to complete the power move. This move is useful if 4's guard is sagging or if he is playing very tightly. If he is sagging, 5's roll off the screen will still be effective. If he is playing tightly, then 4 may be able to drive off the screen and make it all the way to the basket. In either case, 4 has the option to jump shoot over the screen. Diagram 3-27 illustrates.

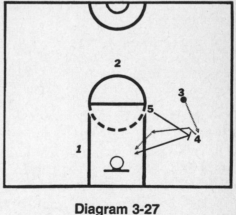

Diagram 3-27

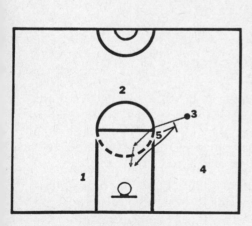

Diagram 3-26

Picking to Start the Offense

If 2 and 3 are having trouble starting the offense with the shuffle pass, then 3 may drive the ball to the outside of 2 as seen in Diagram 3-28. By going outside of 2, 3 keys the pick-and-roll rather than the weave. Player 2 steps over to screen for 3, and 3 now has a good set of options. He can drive to the basket, he can pass to 2 rolling down the key or he can pass to 1 to initiate the shuffle. The chief difference now is that there will be no shuffle cut since there is no one at the strong-side guard position. Player 2 who rolled down the key exits behind 1 as though he had made the shuffle cut. Player 3 screens down for 5 and 4. It should be noted here that a quick pass from 3 to 1 will arrive in time to be relayed to the rolling 2.

Diagram 3-28

The Clear-Out Series

When either 2 or 3 find that they can beat their defensive player one-on-one, they should exercise a clear-out option. These options can be particularly effective if the defensive player has been getting help from teammates sagging over to him.

Diagram 3-29 shows the post, 5, clearing so that 3 can take his defensive player one-on-one. Notice that 2 flares over to his right and that 4 pulls out toward the sideline; this is for double purpose. First, by moving away from 3, they give him more room to operate. Secondly, if 3 is unable to beat his guard, he may pass to 4 who looks for

the shuffle-cutting 2 as seen in Diagram 3-30. This movement pre-
serves the continuity of the offense while allowing 3 to free-lance a
bit.

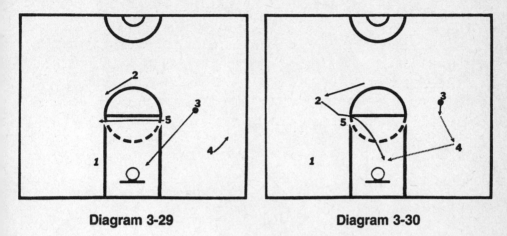

Diagram 3-29   **Diagram 3-30**

Diagram 3-31 shows 1 clearing the side for 2. Player 4 is chased
out front by the clearing of 1, which keeps the balance for continuity
of the offense. If 2 doesn't go all the way to the basket, then he should
be in the number 1 position so that he can pass to the shufffle-cutting
3. Player 4 screens down for 5 and 1 to maintain continuity.

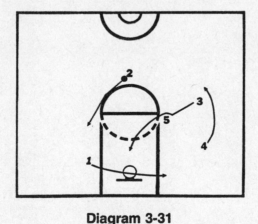

Diagram 3-31

The Double Clear-Out

A nice free-lance clear-out play that is very effective because it is
so quick in developing is illustrated in Diagram 3-32. Player 3 has the

ball, and both 4 and 5 clear out, giving him plenty of room to work. Meanwhile, 4 and 5 screen for 1 and 2 respectively so that they break to the basket in the event that the drive by 3 is stopped.

These are some of the free-lance moves that have worked well in conjunction with the shuffle. They are popular with many coaches who like the shuffle because they afford flexibility and continuity at the same time. This is something not easy to find in offenses, but something that coaches look for.

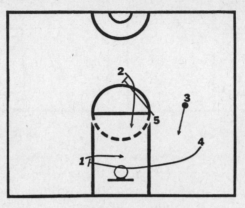

Diagram 3-32

4

*Coaching
the Shuffle
with Drills*

The shuffle pass and the shuffle cut, together with the pair of down-screens by the point guard constitute the basic elements of the traditional shuffle. Some post plays will also be used, depending upon upon which options are used to complement the basic shuffle attack. The shuffle offense is easily taught by practicing and perfecting these elements before combining them into the continuous pattern.

Since all players must be able to play each of the positions within the offense, all should be well drilled in each of the basics, including post play. Players who would not normally play the post, but who occasionally do so in the shuffle find that they have a great advantage if they have practiced their moves, because the defensive players guarding them will probably not be accustomed to defending the post.

When to Use the Drills

The drills for coaching the shuffle should begin at the very beginning of the season and be mastered to the point that they can be well executed by all of the players while not facing any defense. They should be continued throughout the season and practiced diligently to perfect execution and hone offensive timing and reaction. The drills can be readily made more difficult by engaging the players with realistic defense. They can be made more functional by allowing the defense to cheat, thereby helping the offense to read the defensive cheating.

Usually, the most basic passing drills and cutting drills should be taught first since they are the heart of the primary offense and since the timing for them is critical to the success of the offense. It will take only a day or two for the players to learn to execute these fairly well, and then the drills for the down-screens can be added. After that, the offense itself can be taught, using all five players and no defense. You will want to use your own discretion regarding the insertion of drills for post play, but they will generally be inserted after the basic offense has been grasped, as will the addition of rebounding drills.

Great flexibility exists for the use of the passing and cutting drills. Some of them can be omitted or reinstituted, depending on how rapidly the players learn their proper execution. Because the timing between the shuffle pass and the shuffle cut is so essential to the success of the offense, you will want to practice them together.

These passing and cutting drills may easily be inserted as part of the warm-up period at the beginning of practice, as part of the ball handling drills or with lay-ups or other shooting drills. Such use provides daily practice for the players and opportunity for your evaluation.

Passing Drills for Shuffle Offense

The Guard-to-Guard Pass

Diagram 4-1 illustrates a drill for coaching the initial shuffle pass. Using the same numbering system to designate the player positions, players are placed in two lines. One line, designated by 2's in the diagram, forms behind the point guard position with the player who is at the head of the line two steps beyond the top of the foul circle and in direct line with the basket. The players lined up behind the strong-side guard's spot, designated by 3 in the diagram, are even with those in line 2 but midway between the foul lane and the sideline.

The details of the drill are simple but need to be well executed. The player at the head of line "3" dribbles to the foul-line extended with his outside hand, here the left. As he approaches this point, 2 takes a couple of steps to the basket and returns a step by stopping, pivoting and pushing off his outside foot (in this case it is the right foot). As 2 pivots to come back, 3 passes overhead to the outside shoulder of 2. This is done most effectively if 3 has used a two-footed jump-stop and pivots on his right foot to secure a good passing angle to 2. Player 2 should not have to wait for the pass, but should receive it immediately upon completion of his move to clear himself. The details of this drill are simple but the timing is very important and must be practiced. Players should alternate lines during the course of this drill.

This passing drill should be practiced from both sides of the floor. Appropriate adjustments will have to be made in footwork for proper execution from the other side of the floor.

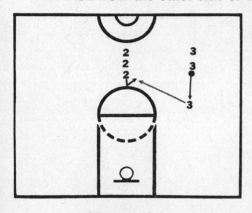

Diagram 4-1

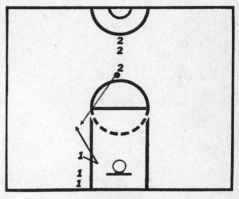

Diagram 4-2

The Guard-to-Forward Pass

Diagram 4-2 illustrates the drill for teaching the second half of the shuffle pass, the guard-to-forward pass. The ball is at the front of line 2 and is passed to the player at the front of line 1 who has placed himself one step out of the key and one step above the block-shaped hash mark. Before the pass is made, 1 must move to the basket a couple of steps and then come back outside to receive the pass. This move outside is made by pivoting toward the ball on his baseline foot (here the right foot) and pushing toward the outside off the same foot.

The pass itself is an overhead pass by 2. It is made by pivoting slightly on the right foot for this pass to the right side of the floor. Player 2 must not make player 1 wait for the ball but must insure that a crisp pass arrives to the outside shoulder of 1 immediately upon the completion of 1's move. Players should alternate lines during the practicing of this drill.

This drill should be practiced to the left side of the floor as well with the proper footwork corrections made.

Back-Door Drill for the Guard

Using the same drill alignment as in Diagram 4-1, Diagram 4-3 illustrates the back-door pass from 3 to 2. The pass is made by 3, who uses the same techniques of jump-stop, right-footed-pivot and overhead pass. The player at the head of line 2 must take his two steps to the basket, pause with right foot forward (for this side of the floor), as if to return to the outside, but then he must accelerate to the basket off the right foot. The pass must reach 2 by the time he completes a running step below the foul line. In order to emphasize the necessity of the early back-door pass, place a coach or manager at the spot marked C in the diagram. If the pass is not made soon enough, then C, who is playing the defensive post, will be able to deflect the ball. Players should alternate lines and practice this drill from both sides of the floor.

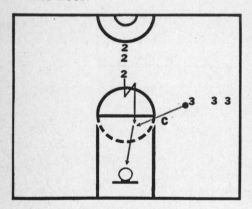

Diagram 4-3   **Diagram 4-4**

Back-Door Drill for the Forward

Diagram 4-4 depicts a drill that teaches the option for the back-door from the shuffle pass to the weak-side forward.

The players divide themselves into two lines as they did in Diagram 4-2. In fact, the drill is conducted as in Diagram 4-2 except that the player at the head of line 1 starts back-door, hesitates on his baseline foot and then accelerates across the key. Player 2 passes the ball overhead to 1 in the key who shoots the reverse lay-up. This drill should be practiced from both sides of the floor by the players, who alternate lines.

Three-Man Shuffle Pass Drill

Diagram 4-5 depicts the drill that combines all of the elements of the four previous drills. Players align themselves at points 3, 2 and 1 as seen in the diagram. Player 3 enters the ball on the dribble and passes to 2, who passes to 1. The fundamentals are the same except that 1 must begin his cut to the basket as 3 passes to 2 in order that the timing be correct. This drill is essential to teach the timing needed for the success of the shuffle pass. It needs to be practiced by all players at all positions and on both sides of the floor.

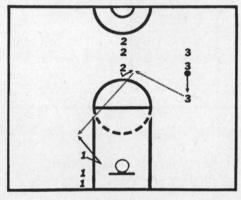

Diagram 4-5

Adding Defense to the Passing Drills

Once the players have perfected the techniques and the timing necessary for the completion of the shuffle pass, then any or all of the previous drills should be practiced against an active man-to-man defense. This enables the players to maintain their timing and learn to read the defense at the same time. It will become imperative that the players cut back-door to combat defensive cheating and help the passers learn to find their targets while under defensive pressure.

If a player with the ball is being overplayed too severely, he should drive to the basket to keep the situation real and the defense honest.

Drills for the Cutter

The Basic Shuffle Cut

Simultaneous with the beginning of the passing drills, cutting drills should begin. The first of these is seen in Diagram 4-6.

Players line up in two groups, one group at position 1 in the diagram and the other at position 3. The player at the front of line 1 has the ball and awaits the shuffle cut by the player at the front of line 3. A chair can be placed at the post position in the beginning stages of this drill.

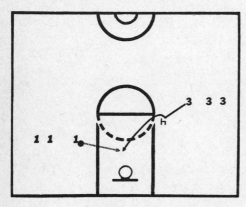   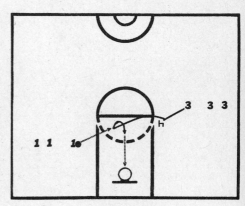

Diagram 4-6   **Diagram 4-7**

Player 3 starts toward the chair at half speed. When he gets to the chair, he plants the outside foot (here the left foot) and pushes off that foot, past the chair in full acceleration to the basket. Player 1 passes to 3 for the lay-up as soon as 1 clears the chair, and the two players exchange lines.

This drill must be practiced to the other side of the floor as well, with the right foot becoming the push-pivot foot for the cutter.

Drill for the Shuffle-Cut and Reverse

Diagram 4-7 shows a drill that is similar to that of Diagram 4-6. The difference is that upon receiving the pass from 1, 3 reverse-pivots in the key for the jump shot. This move is necessary as the lay-up will not be possible every time the shuffle cut is made.

Again, this drill needs to be practiced from both sides of the floor.

Drilling the Shuffle Back-Cut

The drill in Diagram 4-8 practices the shuffle cut to the backside of the post. As in Diagram 4-6, player 3 cuts to the post at half speed, but this time he plants his inside (right) foot, pushes off it to the left side of the post and accelerates to the basket. The player at the head of line 1 passes him the ball as soon as he clears the post, and 3 shoots a right-handed crossover lay-up. Players 3 and 1 exchange lines. Practice this drill from both sides of the floor.

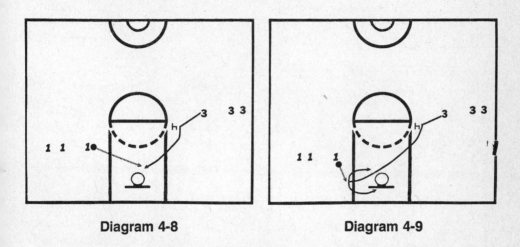

Diagram 4-8   **Diagram 4-9**

Drilling the Baseline Move

Diagram 4-9 shows a move that needs to be practiced when 3 gets the ball too late for the lay-up. Player 3 makes the back-cut as he did in Diagram 4-8, but 1 withholds the ball until 3 has nearly crossed the key. Upon finally getting the ball, 3 power-slides to the basket or reverse-pivots and lays the ball over the rim with the left hand. Both moves need to be practiced from both sides of the floor.

Combining the Passing and Cutting Drills

As can easily be imagined, the drills for the shuffle cut may be combined with those for the shuffle pass. In fact, this must be done sooner or later so that the synchronization of both moves can be perfected. The situation is made more realistic if a post player is added.

Also, when defense is placed at each position, real practice of reading defense begins. The shuffle-cutter must decide which side of the post to cut by, and player 1, as the forward, must decide where he can get the pass to the cutter. The cutter may get the ball very late and have to use one of the moves illustrated in Diagram 4-9.

If the defensive post switches, then 5 must pivot in the opposite direction and roll to the basket as in Diagrams 4-10 and 4-11.

If the defensive guard on 3 cheats behind the post to wait for 3, then 3 must yell "Cheater!" so that player 2 can reverse the ball to 3 for the jump shot over the top of 5. Players should rotate counterclockwise and from offense to defense during the course of this drill. (Diagram 4-12)

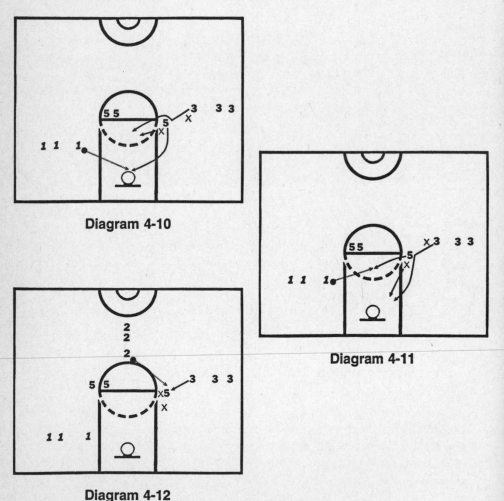

Diagram 4-10

Diagram 4-11

Diagram 4-12

Screening Drills

The screening in the shuffle is rather limited and easy to teach. The basic screen is the down-screen by the point guard for the post and for the strong-side forward.

The most difficult of the two is the screen for the post because of the switching that is apt to occur, and because the screen must occur in the key.

Diagram 4-13 illustrates this screen in drill form. Player 2 shuffle-passes to 1, hesitates one count and then begins the down-screen. The one-second hesitation allows time for 3 to complete his shuffle cut the needs to be practiced. After the hesitation, 2 approaches 5 and sets a screen at a 45-degree angle that has him looking into the left-hand corner of the floor.

The screen is a two-footed jump-screen that must be practiced so that 2 doesn't collide with the defense and cause a foul. He leaves the floor on one foot and lands next to the defensive player on two feet. After alighting, he hesitates and then continues out of the key. Player 5 begins his move as 2 leaves the floor at the beginning of the jump-screen; he cuts past 2, as 2 lands, to receive the pass from 1 for the jump shot. The players rotate counterclockwise during the practice of this drill.

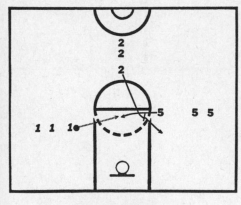

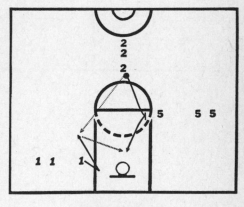

Diagram 4-13   **Diagram 4-14**

Diagram 4-14 shows a drill that teaches reaction to early switching by the defensive guard who tries to stop the jump shot by 5. Player 2 alights on both feet in his screening position, reverse-pivots on his baseline foot, and wheels to the basket. Player 1 passes him the ball.

The complete down-screen is seen drilled in Diagram 4-15. Player 2 passes to 1, jump-screens for 5 and continues on to jump-screen for 4. Player 1 may pass to either 5 or 4. It is important that 2 screen for both players and that both 5 and 4 continue to their new positions following the screen if they fail to get the ball. This helps teach them the shuffle's continuity. Players rotate from 5 to 4 to 2 to 1 to 5 during the course of this drill.

A screening drill for the post screen is important for the utilization of several shuffle options. It is helpful for all of the players to drill this screen-and-roll option from the post position so that they can be thinking of it in the real game situations. Diagram 4-16 illustrates the post stepping out to screen for 3 and then rolling to the basket. This drill should be practiced with defenders on 3 and 5. Also, 5, at the post, can screen for 2 or 4 in similar drills.

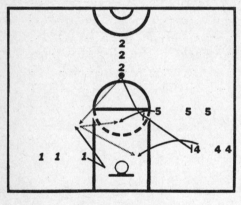

Diagram 4-15

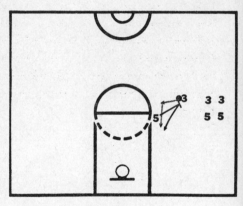

Diagram 4-16

Drills for the Post

The chief drills for the normal shuffle moves of the post have already been illustrated as parts of other drills, These are the post-roll against defensive switching (Diagrams 4-10 and 4-11), the jump shot off the down-screen (Diagram 4-13) and the screen-and-roll option just mentioned. (Diagram 4-16)

However, a number of other good moves should be practiced in conjunction with the running of some of the shufffle options.

The first of these drills is the power-slide off the strong-side entry, which is seen in Diagram 4-17. To start the strong-side entry, 3 passes to 4. Now 5 slides down the lane to get the ball for the power move to the basket. This move assumes that the defensive guard on 5 is playing alongside or in front of 5 as seen in Diagram 4-17.

If the guard is directly behind 5, then 5 makes the same move until he has the guard deep enough so that 4 may pass the ball to 5. Player 5 can now reverse-pivot over the guard and drive to the basket. This latter move is shown in Diagram 4-18.

Both drills should be practiced to both sides of the floor by all players.

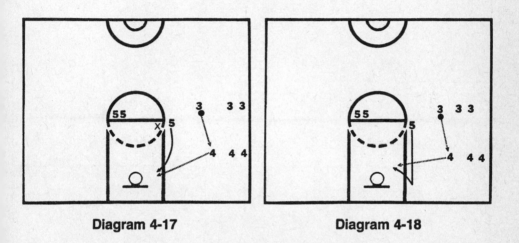

Diagram 4-17   Diagram 4-18

Rebound Drills

A sound theory of rebounding in the shuffle offense is as follows. When a shot is taken, 1 and 4 rebound the sides from the forward positions, 5 rebounds the short middle from the post position, and the ball-side guard rebounds the long middle. The guard opposite the ball is the defensive safety. The basic rebounding can be seen in Diagram 4-19 where 3 is the long rebounder and 2 is the safety.

The basic drill for coaching rebounding is for you to shoot the ball from one side or the other while the offensive players try to rebound against the defense. For this first drill, rebound position is the most important thing, and you should check to see that all four rebound positions are filled along with the safety position.

Diagram 4-20 illustrates the ball being shot from the right side of the floor and the correct offensive rebound reaction. Diagram 4-21 shows the similar situation from the left side. Players should be rotated to different positions and from offense to defense during the practice of these two drills so that they learn the rebound responsibilities of each position on the floor. This is important since all players must be able to play all positions of the shuffle.

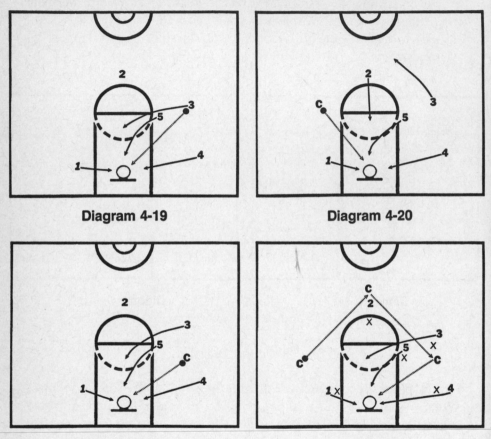

Diagram 4-19   Diagram 4-20

Diagram 4-21   Diagram 4-22

Once the players have learned their basic rebounding responsibilities, anticipation becomes important. Since the defense has the inside position, the offense must anticipate when a shot will be taken so that they can move to the basket ahead of the defense.

Diagram 4-22 shows a good drill for the initial teaching of anticipation in rebounding. Offensive players assume their positions in the shuffle offense alignment. Defensive players each guard one of them.

Three coaches or managers pass the ball on the perimeter of the offense until one takes a shot. The offensive players try to anticipate the shot and try to at least get alongside a defensive player.

The next step is to rebound out of the offense while it is in operation. Begin the shuffle with the offense being guarded by an active defense. Do not pass to cutters until a shot is to be taken and use that key to try to get rebound position on the defense. This drill also teaches the continuity of the shuffle, ball control, and ball handling skills. It can also have defensive emphasis on specific positions if desired.

These are the basic drills that can be used to teach the shuffle. You may wish to add your own drills to this battery. Some coaches have adapted variations of these drills to use as a main part of their pre-practice and pre-game warm-up. This practice is worthwhile since it provides maximum use of practice time to perfect the shuffle, especially its continuity, which is, after all, its strongest feature.

PART II

THE TRIPLE STACK

5

Coaching the Unique Triple Stack Offense

Since developing this offense I have had the opportunity to view some offenses that operate from the triple stack formation. I had seen some scoring plays that utilized the triple stack formation prior to working with the offense. Using the formation as a spring board, our coaching staff experimented with it and came up with a surprisingly potent offense as a result. To the best of my knowledge, this offense is original, unique and got its start on our practice floor several years ago.

We liked the offense immediately. Our players liked it and won with it. In analyzing the offense, we were most impressed by the power that it generates close to the basket. The triple stack offense produces good, open shots quickly while it keeps key rebounders in good rebounding position.

The triple stack offense is included because it is a powerful offense that blends well with the other offenses in this book. It has basic continuity similar to the shuffle offense, yet portions of the triple stack are rule oriented. Part of its motion is like the shuffle, and at times it seems to resemble the 1-4. These similarities make it possible to use the triple stack exclusively or to use parts of it with other offenses in this book.

Before discussing the offense further, here are the advantages and disadvantages of the triple stack offense.

Advantages of the Triple Stack

1. The triple stack is easy to teach and easy to learn.
2. The triple stack is a quick-hitting offense. It doesn't require a great deal of ball handling before producing the good shot.
3. The triple stack produces high-percentage shots at 12 feet or closer. It gets the ball inside and it is not a perimeter offense.
4. It makes very good use of one or more good-shooting big men.
5. The triple stack makes good use of good-driving/good-shooting forwards or guards. It naturally clears a whole side of the floor for them to work one-on-one.
6. The triple stack offense works well against zone defenses as well as man-to-man. Its natural overload is an asset against zones.

Disadvantages of the Triple Stack

1. The triple stack attack may not move the post players enough to suit you; the posts are chiefly screeners and rebounders.
2. The triple stack's power series is a series of scoring plays and not part of the offense's continuity. This lack of continuity may be seen as a disadvantage. However, I have always felt that the good shots generated by the power series more than compensated for the loss of continuity.

The Basic Formation

The triple stack may be set to either side, a flexibility that prevents the defense from anticipating what the offense will do next. However, the alignment in Diagram 5-1 is the one used most and is called the primary formation. In the primary formation, the triple stack is set on the left side of the floor. This is beneficial since the first movement of the offense will be from left to right to aid right handers enroute to the basket. P5, the low post, sets up at the block-shaped hash mark on the left side of the key. He should be a half step out of the key area to insure that he doesn't violate the three-second rule. Ahead of him are the forward on the side, F4, and the high post, P3. They, too, are a half step out of the key, but they vary their position depending upon the defensive reaction to the alignment. If the defense tries to play between them in any way, they should move closer together on the initial set. If the defense is content to remain on the inside of them, they should spread out slightly to make the stack longer.

The right-side forward takes up an initial position that is a step outside of the key and a step above the "block." The point guard usually brings the ball to the offense and should penetrate at least to the top of the key to start the offense.

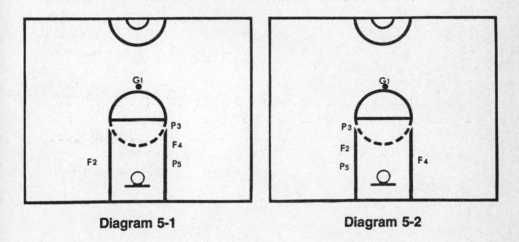

Diagram 5-1   Diagram 5-2

The Secondary Formation

Diagram 5-2 shows the secondary formation set to the right side of the floor. P5, the low post, is at the "block" and a half step outside of the key. Ahead of him are the forward to that side, F2, and the high post, P3. As the reader has determined by now, the change of sides from primary formation to secondary formation is simply made by the posts setting on the right side of the floor instead of the left side of the floor.

The left forward, now the weak-side forward, moves out a bit and up a step as G1 enters the ball to the top of the foul circle.

In a later section the keys will be given that determine whether the primary formation or secondary formation will be used. Unlike the shuffle which keeps the same pattern for each side of the floor, the triple stack has a different pattern for each side of the floor.

Personnel Requirements

Both of the patterns of the triple stack that were just described depend on the pick-and-roll, one high and outside and one low and inside. Each of the screen-and-rolls is done by either P3 or P5, the posts. For this reason, it is desirable that P3 and P5 have some height as the screen-and-rolls are designed to utilize this size. However, in our years of experimentation with the offense we did use smaller players at the post positions and realized success, as long as the two players were adept at the screen-and-roll and were good rebounders. Beyond these considerations, P3, the high post should be the better shooter and, perhaps, the most agile. P5 need only be a rugged, fundamentally sound post player who utilizes his height to advantage.

The pivotal player in this offense, as far as its ultimate success or failure is concerned, is F4, the left forward. He needs to be the best all around player on the team, capable of driving, passing to the roller and scoring from 15 feet out with marked consistency.

The point guard, G1, should be an accomplished ball handler since he is the lone guard and must bring the ball into the offense, often under pressure. G1 can be a real boon to the offense if he is a good jump shooter.

Personnel Placement

As previously indicated, the taller players should occupy the post positions. At least, the posts should be good rebounders and screeners. The high post, P3, should be the better shooter because he operates farther from the basket. Conversely, P5 should be the better rebounder because he is closer to the basket.

The best shooter and driver on the team is F4. His outside shooting threat is necessary to the success of the offense. He is on the left side of the floor so that he will be going to his right, regardless of whether the offense is set to the right or left.

It is nice if the right forward should happen to be left handed so that he would always be going to his left. Since this will probably not be the case, F2 is usually picked after the other slots on the team are filled. He will not usually be the best ball handler since this type of player will become G1. However, a tall guard is preferred since he can work one-on-one from the weak side and use his size to rebound. A short forward could become F2 for similar reasons. We have even placed a player with poor ball skills at that position, and as long as he could move well without the ball, it put great pressure on the defense.

Moves That Key the Offense

The operational movement of the triple stack offense is keyed in three ways: by the side of the floor that the stack is set on, by hand signals and by defensive reactions. With the exception of the shuffle option which occurs later in this chapter, the options that are governed by the defensive reaction will be discussed in Chapter 7. The portion of the offense that is keyed by hand signals is discussed in Chapter 6. The rest of the offense is keyed by setting up in either the primary formation or in the secondary formation. These sets are determined by the high post, P3.

Because P3 is at the high post, he is visible to all of the other players. He is in front of the low post and the forward on his side so that they can see him easily. He is facing the point guard and the forward on the opposite side of the floor. This visibility is the reason that P3 is used to determine the offensive set.

He does so by merely setting up a high post on the left side if he wishes to use the primary formation or on the right side if he wishes the secondary formation. When P3 comes down the floor and assumes a high-post position, P5 and the forward on the corresponding side line up behind him; the opposite forward adjusts his position to become properly aligned for the weak-side position. By this time G1 has penetrated to the top of the key and is ready to begin the offense.

The Weak-Side Pass

Initially, the point guard looks to start the offense with the weak-side pass. It is desirable, but not mandatory, that the ball be passed weak-side, because the side is cleared out for the forward, F2, to work one-on-one with the ball or without it. Diagram 5-3 illustrates. G1 has brought the ball to the top of the key on the dribble. As he nears the top of the key, both F2 and F4 make their initial moves. F4 steps out of the stack to a position outside and slightly above that of

P3. F2 moves to the basket on a genuine cut. G1 looks for F2 first. If F2 has beaten his defensive player, G1 passes him the ball as seen in Diagram 5-3.

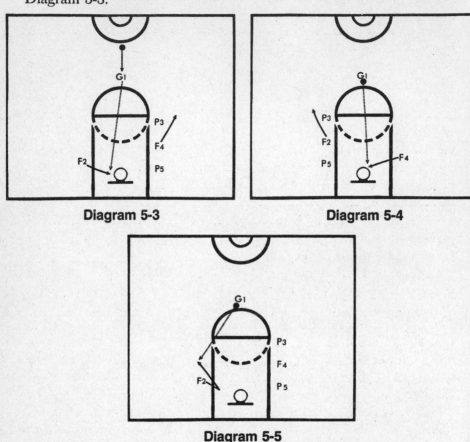

Diagram 5-3   Diagram 5-4

Diagram 5-5

While the previous action was shown in the primary formation, the initiation of the offense is the same in the secondary formation. In Diagram 5-4 the back-door pass from G1 to F4 is shown. F2, the right-side forward, steps out of the stack at nearly the same time.

If the weak-side forward, either F2 or F4 depending on the formation, determines that he will not be able to beat his defensive player on the back-door move, he reverses quickly on his outside foot, pivots toward the ball and breaks outside. F2 so illustrates in Diagram 5-5; F4 would have made the corresponding move had the secondary formation been used. The continuity of the offense really begins with the pass to the forward as he breaks to the outside. We must asssume that if the forward had received the ball during his back-door cut to the inside he would have been close enough that he should shoot, thereby eliminating the need for further continuity.

The Resulting Shuffle

When the ball is passed to F2, who has just moved to the outside, the offense becomes the shuffle as seen in Diagram 5-6. F4, who has just stepped outside of P3, now shuffle-cuts over the top of him for the possible pass from F2. If he fails to get the pass, he becomes the low post on the right side. P3, the high post, rolls to the basket behind F4. If P3 doesn't get the pass, he becomes the high post to the other side as in the big-man shuffle offense described in Chapter 2. Refer to Chapter 2 for the complete discussion of the continuity of this portion of the offense. During the course of the continuity, G1 and P5 may or may not exchange positions on the back side of the offense, according to your decision.

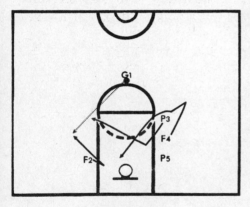 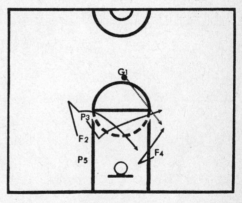

Diagram 5-6   **Diagram 5-7**

Diagram 5-7 illustrates the resulting shuffle that follows a weak-side pass to F4 out of the secondary formation. F2, who stepped out of the stack, shuffle-cuts over the top of P3 to become low post on the opposite side of the key if he doesn't get the ball. P3 rolls behind F2 and becomes, eventually, the high post to the opposite side. The continuity of the big-man shuffle is thus maintained.

To capsulize this section: Any weak-side pass in the triple stack offense that doesn't result in an immediate try for goal, initiates the big-man shuffle.

The Strong-Side Pass from the Primary Formation

If G1 determines that he dares not pass to the weak-side forward, then he looks to the strong-side forward stepping out from behind P3. Because of the nature of the triple stack alignment and the natural defensive reaction to it, the strong-side forward will always be open. He may have to delay his move a bit until G1 has had time to look at the weak-side forward, or the players in the stack may have to tighten their alignment to prevent a defensive player from getting in the stack. The only other way that the defense can cheat is to place a defender on the outside of the stack. Upon seeing this latter ploy, the offense should immediately use the power game described in the next chapter.

Using the strong-side formation as in Diagram 5-8, G1 passes to F4 who has timed his move to the outside so that he will be open after G1 has had the opportunity to look for F2. F4 now works with P3 who sets a screen for him. F4's first option is the jump shot over P3; the second option is the drive past P3's screen and the resulting roll to the basket by P3. Diagram 5-8 shows the drive over the top of P3. Because of defensive cheating, F4 may be able to drive below P3 occasionally, that is, between P3 and P5. P5, in either case, rolls to the outside to an open area that will have resulted from the screen-and-roll.

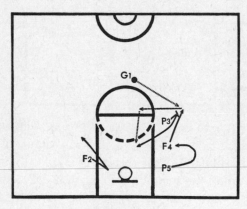

Diagram 5-8

Continuity for the Primary Formation

Should F4 not be able to score or pass to the rolling P3, he then looks for P5. Many times P5 will be able to get open by looping to the outside as seen in Diagram 5-8. If not, however, P5 is to break into the key, trying to secure post position for the pass and a subsequent move to the basket. (Diagram 5-9) If P5 is unable to get any sort of pass, then he moves across the key to become the high post. P3, who rolled through the key previously, now occupies the low post position. The resulting formation is the secondary formation, and F4 still has the ball. F4 now returns the ball to G1 at the point.

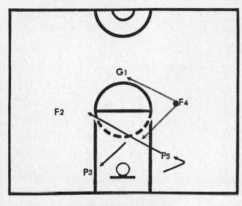

Diagram 5-9

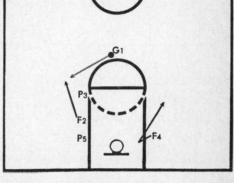

Diagram 5-10

The Strong-Side Pass from the Secondary Formation

Diagram 5-10 shows the ball being returned to the point and the subsequent back-door move to the basket by F4. If G1 fails to find F4 open, F4 steps outside, as shown, and F2 steps out of the stack. G1 now has the option of passing to either F4 to start the shuffle or F2 to begin the triple stack offense from the secondary formation.

A pass to F2 does not begin the same offensive movement that a pass to F4 did in the primary formation. The movement of the offense from the secondary formation is different, regardless of whether the offense started from the secondary formation or it was a continuation of the previous primary offense.

Diagram 5-11 illustrates a pass from G1 to F2 to initiate the secondary offense. P5, the new high post, slides toward the baseline while facing the ball for a pass from F2. This pass is secure and can be completed with ease every time. P3, meanwhile, steps out to screen for P5 who has now begun to dribble toward the junction of the key and the baseline. Using the screen, P3 tries to turn the corner and power-slide to the basket. He should be able to do so, or be able to shoot the jump shot off the screen unless the defense switches.

If the players defending P5 and P3 switch, P5 leans the upper part of his body out of bounds to protect a bounce pass with his right hand to the rolling P3. If P3 executed his screen-and-roll properly, he will be moving into the key with his defender at his back. Following a pass from P5, he should have an uncontested shot. The only player who should have a chance of defending P5 is the player defending against F4. This would, however, leave F4 alone and free to break to the basket for a pass from either P5 or P3. This action is illustrated in Diagram 5-12.

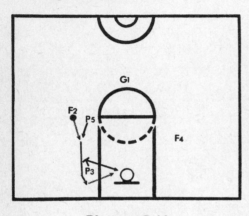
Diagram 5-11

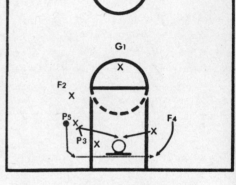
Diagram 5-12

Continuity for the Secondary Formation

If none of the previous opportunities were available to P5, then he should look for F2 coming back to the ball. F2 then passes to G1 who has cleared himself to receive the ball. Previously, P3 rolled through the key following his screen for P5. P3 now becomes the new high post in the primary formation and P5 becomes the new low post after he passes the ball and crosses the key. Diagram 5-13 illustrates this.

Thus, the movement of the secondary formation is completed, and Diagram 5-14 shows the offense in the primary formation once more. G1 has just received the ball and looks for the back-cutting F2 who will pivot and break to the outside if he didn't get the ball on the back-cut. At the same time, F4 steps out of the stack to invite the pass from G1.

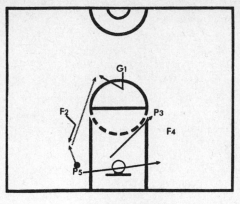

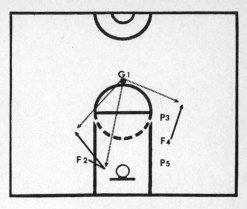

Diagram 5-13   **Diagram 5-14**

The Continuity of the Triple Stack Offense

The triple stack is really two offenses, each with its own continuity. Using the options open to G1 in Diagram 5-14 to illustrate, G1 can pass to F2 upon F2's move to the outside, or he can pass to F4 as he steps outside. If the pass should go to F2, F4 would shuffle-cut and initiate the shuffle offense. The continuity for the shuffle offense is that of the big-man shuffle of Chapter 2. The shuffle and its continuity are to be run any time that the pass is made outside to the weak-side forward in either the primary formation or the secondary formation.

Returning to Diagram 5-14, if G1 had passed to F4, then the triple stack continuity would have been initiated. F4 would have exercised all of the options available to him as described in the section on the continuity of the primary formation. Finding no scoring opportunities, F4 returns the ball to the point, and the offense is in secondary formation. If the ball is not passed to F4 to begin the shuffle but rather goes to F2 coming out of the stack as in Diagram 5-10, then F2 passes to the high post who works with the low post to exercise all of the options of the secondary formation as described in the previous section. When all of these options are exhausted, the offense will be aligned once more in primary formation and ready for the shuffle or for conversion to the secondary formation.

Remember that the triple stack can begin from the secondary formation, explore all of the primary options and become the secondary formation once more.

A Rationale for the Screens in the Triple Stack

Not counting the shuffle rub, two screens are used in the triple stack offense. There is the screen set outside by the high post for the strong-side forward in the primary formation. For review, this screen is shown in Diagram 5-8. There is also the screen by the low post for the high post in the secondary formation. This screen is shown in Diagrams 5-11 and 5-12. The rationale for these screens is based on the premise that most players are right handed, so both screens are set for players who are dribbling to their right.

One screen is set high and to the left, and one is set low and to the right to provide variety.

The screen outside gives the good, all-around ballplayer room and opportunity to apply his skills. It also uses a mobile post as the screener so that a relatively tall player is rolling to the basket.

The inside screen is set close to the basket by one post for another so that their sizes as shooter and roller are used to advantage. It also keeps the least mobile player close to the basket if so desired.

Rebounding the Triple Stack

The rebounding assignments for the triple stack are simple, and one set of rules governs the rebounding responsibilities for the primary formation, the secondary formation and the shuffle.

First, the weak-side forward always rebounds the weak side. Spend time teaching your forwards how to be effective rebounders and it will pay big dividends. Since most of the shots come from the strong side and statistics report that most rebounds fall on the side opposite, aggressive rebounding by the weak-side forward is necessary.

Second, the highest post rebounds the middle, and the lowest post rebounds the strong side (the side that he is on). The reason the rule is so stated is as follows. In Diagram 5-15, for example, if F4 shot over P3's screen in the primary formation, then P3 would be the highest post and would rebound the middle. P5 would rebound his own side, the strong side. But in Diagram 5-16 where P5, who was the high post shoots over a screen provided by P3 and where P3 rolls to the key, then P3 will be the highest post even though he began as the low post.

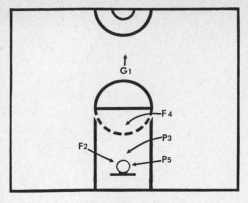

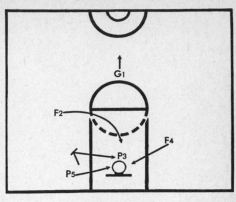

Diagram 5-15   **Diagram 5-16**

Third, the strong-side forward always rebounds the long middle. This rule will provide a long rebounder for the shuffle, too, so long as it is remembered that as soon as he shuffle-cuts, he is the low post; the weak-side forward has become the strong-side forward with the arrival of the shuffle-cutter.

Finally, the point, G1, has to maintain defensive balance by staying outside as safety.

This completes the presentation of the basic triple stack offense, part of which is, admittedly, the big-man shuffle. It is a potent attack, especially with the addition of the power series presented in the next chapter. The shuffle provides the basis for ball-control offense; the power series provides the quick-hitting attack to make the offense complete.

6

Implementing the Power Series

During the course of our experimentation with the triple stack offense, we discovered a couple of plays that we liked very much. We still like them, and the reason is simple; they work. Every time that we have run them, they have produced exactly the shot we wanted. They have never been thwarted to our knowledge.

I am not so naive as to believe that we invented the perfect offense, but I have never seen it stopped. Part of the reason is, I am sure, that when run with the triple stack, the triple stack keeps the defense honest.

Based on the instant success that we received from these two plays, we definitely wanted them to be a part of our offense. The only drawback that we could find with these two plays was that there was no way that they could be worked into the continuity of the offense. At least, we were unable to find a way that they could be worked in without sacrificing the triple stack's simplicity.

Our solution was to keep the plays as scoring plays and not try to combine them into the continuity of the offense. This allowed us to keep the offense intact, to use for ball-control purposes by relying on its continuity, and it gave our offense a new dimension: that of having, not one, but two scoring plays that we could rely on at any time. For obvious reasons, we called them power plays, or power series.

We found that we could set up the triple stack and begin its continuity and then switch to a scoring play from the power series without tipping the defense regarding our intentions. We used the power series every time that we had to have a basket. We used it to end quarters, and we used it to get the last shot of the game when the score was tied. We developed it into 5-second and 10-second scoring plays for those critical late game situations. We inverted it and used it for an inbounds play under our basket. We moved it to the back court and mid-court to insure that we got the ball inbounds against heavy pressure. We even used the power series, or parts of it, in many of these situations, during years when the triple stack was not our primary offense.

We were able to do this without making our plays too complicated. We learned the situation plays as situation plays, and we found that the players learned them quicker and executed them better because they were so similar to a part of our offense. The part of the power series that we used in the regular offense, or whenever we needed to use it, we keyed with a hand signal from the player at the high post. Remembering from the previous chapter that the high-post player keyed the primary formation and the secondary formation because he was so readily visible to the rest of the team, it is easy to see why we used him.

We coached the post players on how to vary the power series with the primary and secondary formations of the triple stack so that the offense had a nice, unpredictable blend of all of them. A rule of thumb that worked well for us: Vary the offensive formation every third time down the floor and vary the play used to start the offense every other time. This means that the primary (because it is the primary) formation gets used twice as often as the secondary. It also means that a different tactic is used offensively each time down the floor. The post must remember that the pass outside to the weak-side forward automatically signals the beginning of the shuffle offense and preempts any other play that the post may have called.

It is now easy to see why and how the triple stack is so varied, making it difficult for the defense to anticipate what is going to happen next.

The Advantages of the Power Series

1. The power series is easy to include with the triple stack offense.
2. Many coaches are experimenting with and finding successful applications of the power series to zone offense.

3. The power series has the advantage of special situation plays that are the same as a portion of the regular offense.

4. The power series generates open shots at a maximum of ten feet from the basket.

5. The power series provides for good rebounding position.

6. The power series provides good scoring opportunities for each post player.

7. The power series can be run from either the primary formation or the secondary formation.

8. Much of the power series can be incorporated with other offenses or styles of play.

Disadvantages of the Power Series

1. As mentioned previously, the only disadvanage of the power series that we could find is that it is difficult to include into the triple stack continuity.

Keying the Power Play for the High Post

As previously mentioned, the power series is easy to key. It may also be run to either side of the floor from either the primary formation or the secondary formation. For purposes of illustration, the power plays used in the regular offense will be shown to the sides that provide them the greatest advantage.

The power play for the high post is best run from the secondary formation as pictured in Diagram 6-1. In Diagram 6-1, G1, the point guard has brought the ball to the top of the key to initiate the offense. P3, the high post who signaled the secondary formation by setting up on the right side of the floor, now signals his power play by holding out his left arm to call for a pass to that spot on his outside. This signal not only gives G1 a passing target, but also gives F2, the strong-side forward, a signal and a barrier to prevent him from breaking to the outside. After looking over F4 and his inside-outside move, G1 passes to P3's target, and P3 receives the ball as he wheels to his left to dribble to the baseline and shoot over the automatic double screen provided by F2 and P5.

The advantages of this play are many. First, it is run from a normal formation. Second, it provides F4, the weak-side forward, opportunity to preoccupy his defender and possibly initiate the offense if the defender failed to respond. Third, the pass from G1 to P3 is a safe pass. Fourth, P3 who is probably right handed will be dribbling and shooting with his right hand on a move from the left. The shot has an excellent angle for P3 to use the backboard and is no further than ten feet from the basket. Finally, there is no way that the defense could have anticipated that this play was going to be run in time to have cheated a defender, whether from the top or bottom, to the outside so as to defend P3.

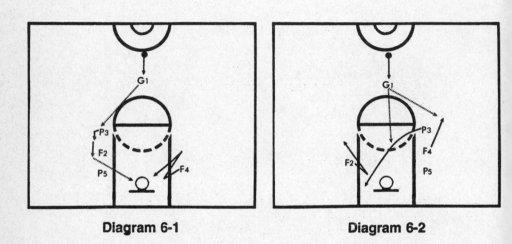

Diagram 6-1   Diagram 6-2

Keying the Power Play for the Low Post

The power play for the low post is best run from the primary formation. Diagram 6-2 illustrates. G1 enters the ball to the top of the key as F2 makes his inside-outside move. Meantime, P3, who signaled the primary formation, signals the power play for the low post by holding out his inside (or left) hand as though he were calling for the ball. To make this feint seem more realistic, P3 breaks to his left, crosses the key as though he were on a power slide to the basket, and finally secures a good rebounding position. F4, meantime, has broken to the outside as he normally does to help initiate the offense. As seen in Diagram 6-2, there will be opportunity for G1 to pass to either P3 inside or F4 outside, and he should do so if either is open. However, F4's defender will be hustling to get outside and defend against an anticipated jump shot by F4. P3 will probably not be open either since he must pass three defenders in the key. He will, however, pull his defensive player toward the opposite side of the key. This leaves P5 and his defender in a vacuum created when everyone left their area. P5, anticipating this, gets on the heels of P3's defender (who is crossing the key in defense of P3) and uses him as a moving screen to the basket. Now it may happen that P5 and his defender will have left the area before the ball arrived. If this is the case, P5 must step to meet the pass and secure a post position on top of his defender in time to receive the ball. The key is now vacant for P5 to work one-on-one. This close to the basket the odds and the rules greatly favor P5, who is probably the tallest offensive player. This power move by P5 is depicted in Diagram 6-3.

On paper, this play appears to be one of those that might receive a quizzical look and then be passed off as doubtful. I continue to be amazed at the repeated success of this play, even against teams that have scouted it or seen it before. The natural reaction, defensively, is to slough against it. Players will automatically adjust to sloughing since it presents a wide-open scoring opportunity for the offense.

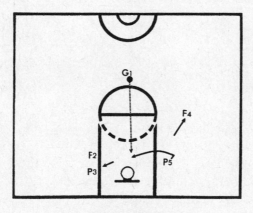

Diagram 6-3

How to Beat the Slougher

In our years of working with the triple stack, we have only seen the slough come from two areas to help defend against this portion of the power series. There are three possibilities to slough help from, but we have only seen it come from two.

The first and most common area to bring help from is to sag the player defending P3 over to help stop P5. This defensive action is seen in Diagram 6-4. The defender left P3 so that the ball can be lobbed to P3 from the point as seen in Diagram 6-4. While the diagram shows the lob, the pass may come at any time during P3's slide across the key. The determining factor will be the slough, that is, how soon P3's defensive player leaves to help guard P5. He cannot leave until P5 actually has the ball, and then he can leave to help effect a double-team on P5 with P5's defender. If this is the case, then the pass to P3 comes from P5 before the double-team can be set as seen in Diagram 6-5.

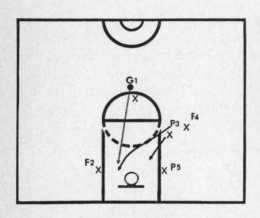

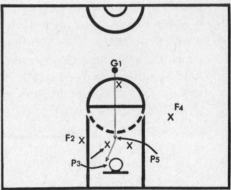

Diagram 6-4   Diagram 6-5

Diagram 6-6 illustrates the slough from another area, in this case from the defender who should be guarding F4. Instead of playing the honest defense on F4 and following him to the outside, this defender stayed to help double-team P5. G1 recognizes this and rifles the ball to F4 who uses P5's stationary screen for the good shot much as P3 did in his power move in Diagram 6-1. Generally F4's defensive player cannot get back to F4 in time to stop this attempt. If anyone is able to get to him, it will usually be P5's defensive player who switched over to cover. This should key a roll to the basket by P5 who now has inside position and height advantage.

For some reason, we have never faced the slough from the weak-side forward. Perhaps the natural clear-out that the weak-side forward has puts enough pressure on his defensive player that he feels compelled to play good, honest defense on him. If, however, his defensive player does switch, the weak-side forward should get the ball for the jump shot, move one-on-one or initiate the shuffle offense.

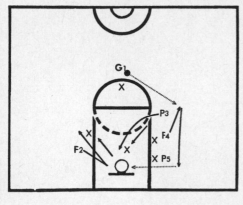

Diagram 6-6   **Diagram 6-7**

Rebounding the Power Series

There is no problem in teaching rebounding for the power series. In fact, the power series provides good opportunity for effective rebounding because it keeps players so close to the basket.

Diagram 6-7 shows good rebounding position for the power play for the low post. Assuming that P5 shot the ball, he is in good position to rebound the ball as the short-middle rebounder. Since everyone left F4's side of the floor, he has become the weak-side forward and rebounds his side accordingly. Conversely, F2 rebounds the long middle as the strong-side forward. P3 rebounds his side of the basket. G1 is defensive safety, as usual.

The notable exception to the rules for rebounding the triple stack occurs during the power play for the high post. The rule that is excepted is the one for the posts, which states that the higher of the two posts is to rebound the short middle. Since P3, the high post, is to shoot the ball over the screens of F2 and P5, there is little hope of him being able to get to the short middle. Our solution is to simply have P3 follow his shot; in effect, become the long-middle rebounder. F2, the strong-side forward, is in good position to rebound the short middle. All other rebounding responsibilities remain the same as Diagram 6-8 illustrates.

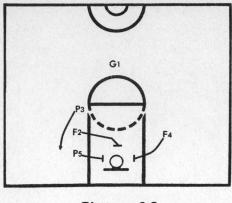

Diagram 6-8

Since the power series is usually added to the basic triple stack offense, the same four people are accustomed to going to the boards so that the above exception to the rebounding rules is not a problem. In fact, the players adapt to it easily.

Using the Power Series to End a Period

Because the power series delivers such good shots, it is ideal to use as time expires during a period of play. It also provides good rebounding for last second tipping should the shot be missed.

If very little time remains in a period of play as the offense brings the ball into front court, the use of the power series becomes ideal because it is so quick-hitting. Do not assume, however, that the players will learn to do this automatically. They must practice it often. The play is not difficult, and they are used to running it. They will not be used to watching for the expiration of time unless it is made important to them through practice. The high post must be especially well drilled to watch the time, to know your philosophy for last second situations, to know who should shoot the ball and when to initiate the play.

If more time exists in a period than is required to run the power series, then the players must also be instructed and practiced regarding correct procedure. What is deemed to be correct will depend on your philosophy and on the game situation. But, assuming that the last shot of the period is desired by the offense and assuming that there is more time left on the clock than necessary for the execution of the power series, then the following strategy is effective. Use the triple stack continuity or the shuffle continuity to produce the sure lay-up and, hopefully, the three-point play until time remaining is less than ten seconds. Once less than ten seconds remains and the offense has not been able to get a lay-up, then complete the continuity cycle, whether it be the shuffle or the triple stack, and initiate the power series immediately. This is easy to do since the offense sets itself for the power series each time it completes a continuity cycle.

Either play from the power series works well to end a period with the last shot.

A 5-Second Play from the Power Series

The triple stack power series provides a good 5-second play for those must situations when the offensive team must score to tie or win the game. The above procedure works well, and sometimes it is to the advantage of the offense to try to set and score without taking time out and then inbounding the ball against a set defense. However, coaching philosophies and game situations may dictate the necessity of a scoring play from the front court sideline with less than six seconds remaining in regulation play.

Diagram 6-9 illustrates a play that has had much success for us. It is essentially the power play for the high post, but from a sideline inbounds pass. G1 inbounds the ball. He needs to be a good passer. If not, insert someone into the line-up who is. I will concede that the play should not work as diagramed. However, I continue to be amazed at the number of defenses which will line up under pressure as shown in Diagram 6-9. If the defense does line up as diagramed, simply rifle the ball to P3, the high post, as he steps behind the double screen for the unmolested shot. F4 crashes his side of the boards while F2 and P5 rebound as soon as their screening responsibilities are finished.

If the defense wishes to, and wisely so, pit five players against four offensive players as the ball is inbounded, then Diagram 6-10 shows the offensive play that works well. G1 again inbounds. However, the close proximity of the defensive player outside of P3 will keep him from getting the ball so he makes sure that everyone knows that he is being defended from the outside. Consequently, F4 breaks across the key so as to provide a pick for P5 who is breaking opposite. G1 now has two options: F4, the good shooter breaking to the ball and

P5, the tall post, in an established position for the lob pass. If the pass comes to F4, then F2 drops down a step or so to provide additional screening for F4 to work around.

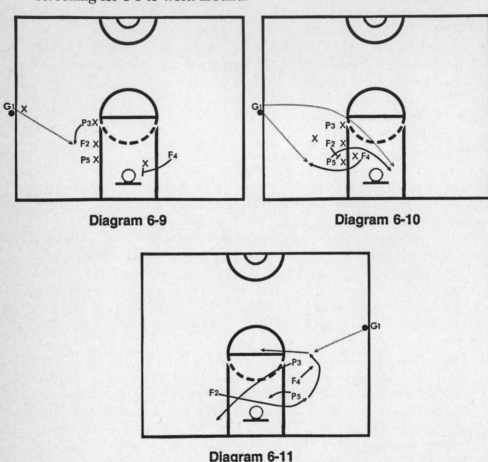

Diagram 6-9   Diagram 6-10

Diagram 6-11

A 10-Second Play from the Power Series

Diagram 6-11 presents a play that requires a bit of time to develop. It has several scoring options that are very effective. Like the previous 5-second plays, it can be run to both sides of the floor. Here we see it initiated from the left sideline.

G1 again inbounds the ball. As the ball is placed in the hand of G1 by the official, F2 breaks around the triple stack, and G1 has the options of passing to him immediately for the jump shot over the triple screen or later so that he may dribble over the top of the screen.

If the pass comes to F2 early and F2 is open, it is important that he shoot. If F2 gets the ball late, then it is important that he drive the ball to the foul line area even if he knows that he will be unable to drive all the way to the basket. As F2 approaches the foul line, P3 initiates the power move for the low post by breaking low and opposite. F4 steps outside, and P5 positions himself for the one-on-one move near the basket. F2 has the options to shoot from the foul line or pass to P3, F4, P5, or G1.

G1 does not stand still after passing F2 the ball as Diagrams 6-12 and 6-13 illustrate. In Diagram 6-12, G1 passes to F2 early and low; he goes opposite F2 by breaking over the top of the stack. Much of the time, he will be open on the weak side following this move. If he passes to F2 high and late, then he breaks opposite and low. He may be open as he clears the bottom of the stack for the pass from G1, or he may be open near the foul line extended as a last resort should the power play fail.

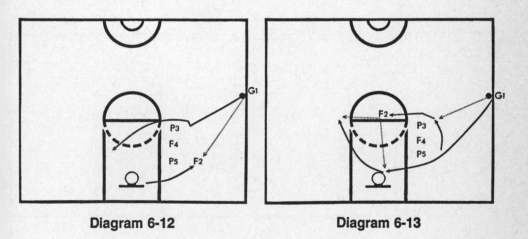

Diagram 6-12   Diagram 6-13

The players should have opportunity to practice this play since their natural reaction will be to rush it. They need to learn that ten seconds can be ample time for the play to develop and produce a good shot.

Power Series Scoring Plays from Under the Basket

By inverting the position of G1, the old stack inbounds play can be converted to the power series. For instance, Diagram 6-14 shows the alignment. It is the same as that of the triple stack offense except that G1 is looking at the offense from under the basket instead of from out front. The play is one of the basic plays of the old stack inbounds plays, except that F4 is on the weak side of the floor instead of in the stack. If the ball should be inbounded from the other side of the floor then F4 would be in the triple stack and F2 would be the weak-side forward. The play is keyed by the defense and is simple. If the defense places no one outside the stack, then the offense executes the power play for the high post by simply stepping P3 outside and down as depicted for the jump shot over the double screen. If the defense places a defender on the outside, then the offense runs the power play for the low post by breaking P5 across the key as an option, stepping F4 outside toward the corner, and breaking P3 to the basket. G1 can now pass to any of the three. The play is a good one because it takes advantage of P5's size, the shooting ability of a good forward like F2 and the size, mobility and shooting of P3. (Diagram 6-15)

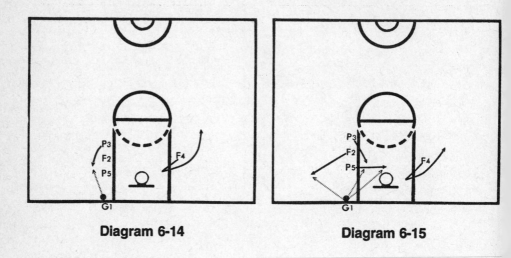

Diagram 6-14   **Diagram 6-15**

F4, the weak-side forward is not neglected as Diagram 6-16 shows. It is surprising how much the defense tends to neglect him, however. G1 should always look to F4 first as he would in the basic triple stack offense. F4 may be open on the back side of the offense for the quick pass or he may be open near the foul line later as the defense sags to protect the middle. At the foul line, F4 is both defensive safety and offensive safety valve for the inbounds pass.

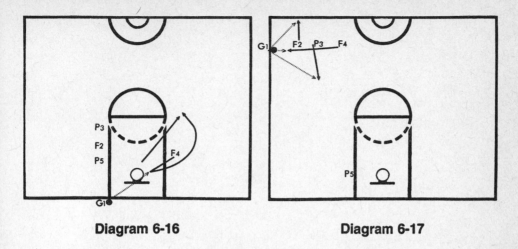

Diagram 6-16   **Diagram 6-17**

Other Inbound Situations and the Power Series

Because the above plays worked so well, we have used the same power series concept to inbound the ball in other situations, most often in our front court when facing heavy pressure. We use an alignment similar to that of Diagram 6-17 when we must get the ball in. G1 inbounds the ball while P5 posts low to keep their post busy. The remaining players line up in a triple stack as shown. The front player in the stack may break either way, while the second player in the stack breaks opposite. G1 should get the ball to either one if they happen to be open. If they are not open, then the pass should go to F4 breaking to the ball. Once the ball is in, return it to G1 and set the offense. Other coaching suggestions for defeating pressure while using the triple stack offense are offered in the next chapter.

Meanwhile, the power series of the triple stack provides potent scoring plays for the entire attack. These plays can be used with the triple stack as shown here to provide a simple and cohesive offensive attack, or they may be combined with other offenses contained in this book.

7

Maintaining
Continuity with
Free-Lance
Options

One of the reasons that I like the triple stack offense so well is that it blends easily with the shuffle. In fact, the shuffle inspired much of our thinking on the triple stack, and it is a built-in portion of our triple stack offense. It is only natural, then, that many of the free-lance options for the shuffle contained in Chapter 3 work well with the triple stack. Specifically, the weave, the pick-and-roll, and the split-the-post options for the shuffle adapt well to the triple stack. These options were described in Chapter 3. The clear-out series also applies well to the triple stack since the natural alignment of the stack automatically clears one whole side of the floor.

All of these free-lance options may be used to help maintain the continuity of the triple stack offense by keeping the defense from cheating. However, these options can be supplemented with or complemented by free-lance options designed especially for the triple stack offense.

The Back-Door for the Weak-Side Forward

Diagram 7-1 depicts a free-lance option that has already been discussed, but it is presented here so that its possibilities may be expanded, especially since the defense will want to cheat here the most often. Normal defensive reaction to the initial triple stack alignment is to encourage the player defending against F2 to overplay him early in the game. The offense will want to counter with the back-door by F2 (or F4 if the offense is in the secondary formation) as seen in Diagram 7-1. This maneuver causes the defensive forward on the weak side to play honestly for a while so that the shuffle options and the one-on-one options may be used.

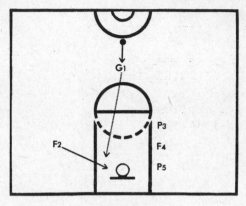

Diagram 7-1

The Triple Screen for the Weak-Side Forward

The weak-side forward's defensive player will begin to shadow the weak-side forward later in the game. Having become accustomed to the constant feint to the basket by the weak-side forward, this defensive player will learn to defend it by going with the feint just far enough so that the back-door pass cannot be made and then drifting to the outside ahead of the weak-side forward so that he cannot get the pass to initiate the offense. At this time the play shown in Diagram 7-2 works very well. The weak-side forward, here F2, makes his customary cut to the basket when G1 has the ball at the top of the key, but continues beyond the basket and around the triple stack to receive a pass from G1. Normally, F2 will have time to take the excellent shot afforded by the triple screen before the defense can recover. However, he does have a number of other options open to him. F2 can drive toward the baseline for the shot or he can execute a pick-and-roll with the low post as seen in Diagram 7-3. This becomes an excellent option if P5's defensive player breaks outside to defend F2. The pick-and-roll should send P5 to the basket with his normal defen-

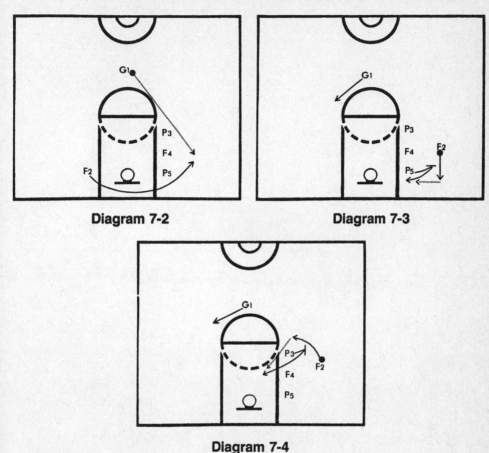

Diagram 7-2

Diagram 7-3

Diagram 7-4

der picked cleanly out of the play and with a much shorter player trying to prevent the shot by F2. Also, the baseline provides nice protection for the pass from F2 to P5 if F2 leans over the line to bounce-pass to the rolling P5.

Of course, F2 may also attempt to drive over the top of the screen as shown in Diagram 7-4. This maneuver works well if F2's defensive player follows him closely around the screen. The natural result to the drive over the top by F2 will be the switch by P3's defensive player to head F2 off as seen in Diagram 7-4. At this point, P3 should roll to the basket.

If none of these options present themselves to F2, he may simply dribble to the point to initiate the offense. While he has the ball at the top of the key, the entire side of the floor that he vacated becomes an excellent one-on-one area for G1 to work through as he moves to the basket to initiate the offense as the new weak-side forward. This action is shown in Diagram 7-5.

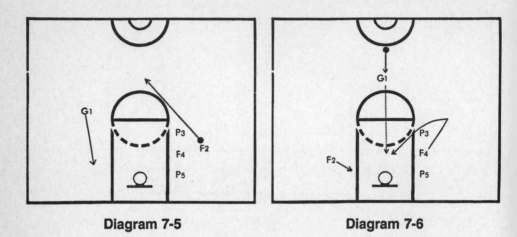

Diagram 7-5   **Diagram 7-6**

An Option for the Strong-Side Forward

An option that works very well for the strong-side forward is shown in Diagram 7-6. Working from the primary formation as shown, F4's defensive player becomes accustomed to waiting for the preliminary move by F2 on the other side of the floor before anticipating a move by F4. This defensive player turns his head to watch F2. He may even actively help defend F2 by stepping into the passing lane to hinder any sort of pass from the point. When this happens, F4 should leave immediately by cutting around P3 as shown. This move will probably precede any move by F2 and will leave F4 open for the jump shot at the foul line or the shorter shot, if he is able to penetrate. He should be encouraged to penetrate, if possible, since this could open P5 near the basket if P5's man switches to cover.

The Low Post Option

Two defensive players will be lulled to sleep by the triple stack offense. They are the players defending the low post and the point guard. The player defending the low post tends to forget his assigned player since he is always the last to move from the stack. He turns his head and helps defend against the slashing cuts by the offense by sloughing toward the middle. The low post, P5, must be taught and encouraged to take advantage of this inattention. He should reverse-pivot and cut behind his guard for the pass from the point as shown in Diagram 7-7, or he can make the same move and post low on the opposite side to the key for the pass from F2 as seen in Diagram 7-8.

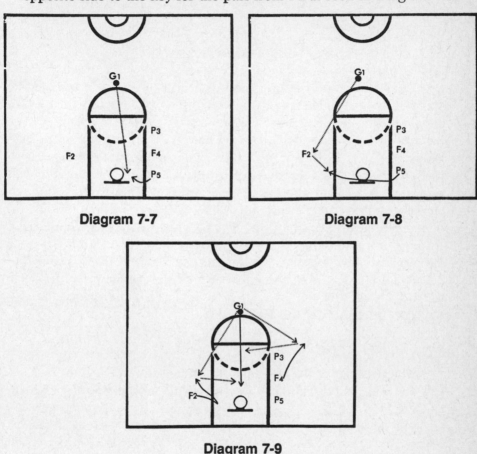

Diagram 7-7   **Diagram 7-8**

Diagram 7-9

The Give-and-Go for the Point Guard

The other player who may tend to become a spectator instead of a defender against the triple stack is the point guard. Since his assigned player at the point does not do a great deal in the offense, he will become lazy and turn to watch the play. When this happens, G1 should execute the give-and-go play in Diagram 7-9. This play may be executed from either F2 or F4, depending on where the first pass went, and it may be executed from either the primary or secondary formation. G1 should cut to the basket whenever his defensive guard turns his head. If he does not get the ball in return, G1 can cut through the key and circle back to the point without disrupting the play in progress. If he cuts around the triple stack, he may be open behind it for the good shot, similar to the move made by F2 in Diagram 7-2.

Defeating Pressure

After facing the slashing cuts and the good inside power shots afforded by the triple stack attack, many teams will try to disrupt the offense before it gets started. In fact, it may be one of the disadvantages of the triple stack that those using it are almost certain to face heavy pressure. However, in these days of sophisticated defenses and well-coached teams defensive pressure is a way of life for high school basketball teams and, therefore, is not unusual. The reason that pressure is discussed here is that the point guard becomes the focal point of the pressure exerted by the defense. As such, preparation may need to be exercised so that he doesn't panic.

One of the defensive ploys is to exert strong overplay on the point guard so that he cannot pass to the side of the floor that the stack is on. This ploy is almost certain to be used if the offense has an exceptional shooter at the F4 position.

The Trap Play for the Point Guard

The overplay at the point guard can be seen in Diagram 7-10, as can the trap play designed to take advantage of the overplay. F2, or

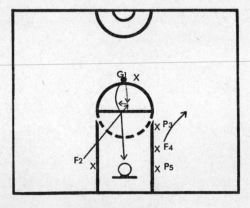

Diagram 7-10

F4 if he should be the weak-side guard, must be conscious of such a possibility. When he sees G1 under strong-side overplay after G1 has picked up his dribble, F2 should break to the foul line to create an open pass for G1. Upon passing the ball, G1 breaks by the weak-side forward, who is now at the foul line. The forward returns the ball to G1 while acting as a post for G1 on which to rub his man off. If the forward's defensive player should switch, the forward should shoot the ball immediately.

A Method of Entering the Ball

If overplaying the point guard fails to work for the defense, they are almost sure to try one of two other strategies.

The first is to utilize a half-court trapping defense to double team the point guard so that he will give up the ball before the offense is in a position to be initiated. The second strategy is to exert full-court pressure on G1 so that he will not be able to handle the ball at all, the theory being that the point guard must have the ball before the offense is able to work. Also, it presumes that since all other players are posts or forwards they will be unable to get the ball to the offensive end without losing it. In either case, let the forwards enter the ball. This works better than the defnese would like to believe. One of the forwards is apt to be the best overall ballplayer and the other is often a guard who has been converted to a forward to fit the requirements of the triple stack. Send the posts to the other end of the floor. This helps in two ways: It keeps a couple of the defensive players occupied so that they are unable to spend too much pressure on the ball handlers, and it helps get the offense started.

The posts cue themselves on whoever has the ball. Assuming that the point guard will not have it, since this is the strategy of the defense, either F2 or F4 will have the ball. If F2 has the ball, the posts align themselves in the primary formation. If F4 has the ball, the posts set in the secondary formation as described in Chapter 5.

For purposes of explanation assume that F2 has the ball as shown in Diagram 7-11. On this cue, the posts have set in the primary formation. G1 and F4 slash toward the basket, but they probably won't get the ball. However, the maneuver forces the defense to relax the outside pressure a bit. F4 takes his place in the stack as shown.

Diagram 7-12 shows the continuation of this play. F4 is now in the stack, and G1 continues his move toward the basket, through the key, and around the triple stack. I feel that it is impossible to defend G1 (or any player stepping out of or around the stack) to the point that he is unable to get the pass from the point. F2 now hits G1 with a pass as shown in Diagram 7-12, and G1 has all of the options open to him that were shown in Diagrams 7-2, 7-3, and 7-4.

If, however, the main objective of this maneuver is to get the offense set with G1 at the point, then G1 may dribble to the point while F2 slashes to the basket to begin the offense as seen in Diagram 7-13. The offense has been able to set itself safely while engaging the defense with several moves toward the basket.

This method of entering the ball works equally well to both sides of the floor.

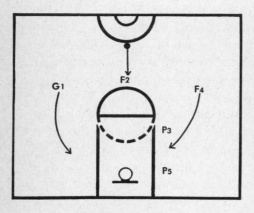

Diagram 7-11

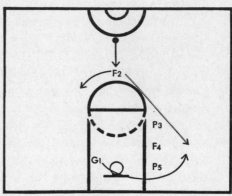

Diagram 7-12

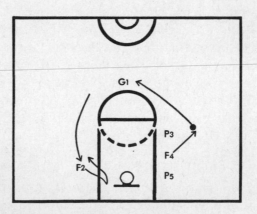

Diagram 7-13

The Dribble Game

Consistent with the preceding discussion about defeating pressure, we borrowed an idea and adapted it to the triple stack as a free-lance offense that could be used to foil defenses that applied too much pressure. We also found that is was a great offense for slowing down a game late in the second half. It is presented here as an alternative for either. It blends very well with the triple stack, the shuffle, the passing game and the 1-4 offense. A team employing this offense can move into its regular offense with ease so that the defense cannot anticipate an impending pattern.

Diagram 7-14 illustrates the beginnings of the dribble game. Here, it is shown set in the triple stack's primary formation. G1 initiates the dribble game by dribbling the ball at F2. This is a nice option that G1 has; it has been previously overlooked in discussions of the triple stack except in passing mention of the pick-and-roll and weave options. This time, it signals a back-door clear-out for F2 who continues on to the other side of the floor if he doesn't get the ball.

F4, meanwhile, breaks out of his stack and rotates to the top of the key. He times his arrival at the top of the key with the arrival of G1 at the weak-side forward position. Simultaneous with the arrival of G1 at the forward position, the high post, P3, loops through the key and exits low. G1 has had the passing options of F2 on the back-door cut, P3 on the loop or F4 breaking toward the ball at the top of the key. If P5 or F2 got the pass, a try for goal should result. If F4 gets the ball, the offense is recycled and can be run again. P5 has moved to the high post, replacing P3 who looped low.

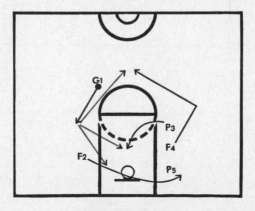

Diagram 7-14

Diagram 7-15 shows the continuity of the free-lance. F4 dribbles at G1 who clears out. P5 loops through the key, and P3 fills high to replace him. F2 breaks toward the ball at the top of the key, timing his arrival with the arrival of F4 at the weak-side forward position.

The dribble game is really two concentric wheels formed by offensive movement. The outer wheel, formed by the point guard and the two forwards, looks to the inner wheel formed by the post players who are sliding to the basket.

Obviously, the dribble game, as presented, is quite simple and really functional. Remeber that this is a free-lance offense that only uses the concentric circles as a basis for continuity and organization. The players individually have options that they should exercise whenever they have opportunity to do so. The first option is that any time the ball is reversed behind the stack by a pass, the dribble game is to be discontinued and the pattern game is to be resumed. Similarly, any time that the point doesn't dribble to chase the weak-side forward to the other side of the floor, the pattern game is to be resumed. Other options follow.

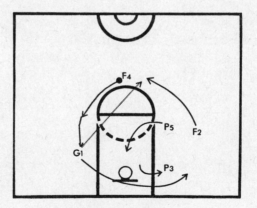

Diagram 7-15

Driving Options for the Dribble Game

Players with the ball must remember that they always have the option to drive to the basket if they find their defensive player out of position or if they are confident that they can defeat their defensive player one-on-one. Since the ball is always in the hands of the point player until he releases it to a new point player, the drive will only come from one side of the floor, that being the area between the point and the weak-side forward as shown in Diagram 7-16. This diagram shows F2 driving. This is only for purposes of illustration. Once G1 dribbles and F2 clears out, then G1 has become the weak-side forward, F2, and is so depicted.

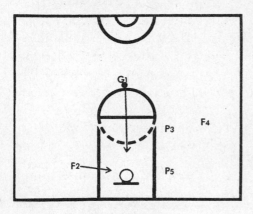

Diagram 7-16

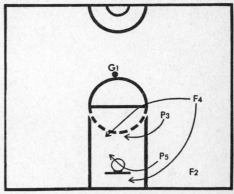

Diagram 7-17

Back-Door Options for the Dribble Game

The back-door options for the dribble game are the most important and the most potent part of the offense. Diagram 7-17 illustrates quick reverses by the posts as they loop back-door. This move by the posts is very effective if they wait until the defensive players are distracted by action on the weak side and then reverse-pivot and cut behind their defensive players. Diagram 7-17 also shows F4 cutting to the basket while using P3 and P5 as posts to scrape away his defensive player. This move is much like the shuffle cut of Part I of this book. The ball will usually be at the weak-side forward position, as in the shuffle cut, although this is not necessary. F4 should make this move regardless of the position of the ball. His only consideration is that he can beat his defensive player.

The Give-and-Go

The give-and-go is always an option that is open to the point guard. If he is at the point, then he may use either F2 or F4 for the give. This may conflict a bit with the regular offense, and coaches may wish to instruct their teams that if the give-and-go should fail, they should continue with the dribble game or change to the regular pattern style of play. This decision will depend upon your philosophy and the makeup of the team.

If the point guard has moved the ball on the dribble to the weak-side forward position, he can also execute the give-and-go with the new point guard when he returns the ball to that position. The nice thing about the attempted give-and-go from the weak side of the floor is that it resembles the pattern triple stack offense so much that the defense is not able to tell the difference and dares not cheat or anticipate.

The Triple Stack and Zone Defenses

Much fertile work will be done in the next few years with the use of triple stack against zone defenses. We have experimented with the triple stack against zones ourselves. We have discussed its possibilities with other coaches and watched their results, and we know that it is being experimented with at the college level. We have had the opportunity to see it work many times against zones, and we are confident that it has much merit.

It is presented here because, as a zone offense, it is a free-lance offense rather than a pattern offense. It does have many various possibilities, perhaps even as a pattern offense against zones. However, we like the unstructured zone attack and consequently prefer to use the triple stack to allow us to get into the seams of the zones and penetrate with the pass or with the drive.

Coaches who use it comment that their best success with the triple stack against zones is on nights when their offense seems to be stymied and they find it difficult to get movement from their players. They find that it is also a good vehicle for adjusting their players to unorthodox zone defenses.

Here are a few of the possibilities of the triple stack presented against a standard 2-1-2 zone. Diagram 7-18 illustrates the power play for the high post as described in Chapter 6. P3 merely holds out his hand to call for the ball and rolls behind the double screen afforded by F4 and P5. F4 and P5 may have to actively screen the middle man in the zone and the baseline defender closest to the ball.

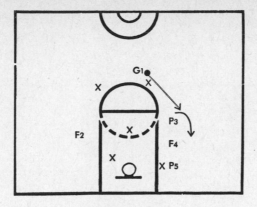

Diagram 7-18

Diagram 7-19 illustrates a similar variation. The low-post player steps up for the pass to the outside of the double screen afforded by P3 and F4. If the baseline defender tries to follow at all, then this option has good possibilities for a roll by F4, who should find it easy to get inside the middle man.

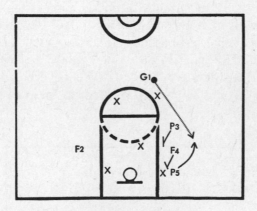

Diagram 7-19

In Diagram 7-20, F4 steps out for the pass from the point while P3 and P5 screen for him. This play has the best possibilities of any presented so far, because F4 will probably be the best shooter while P5 and P3 maintain rebound position. The middle man of the zone dares not go out to defend F4 or else he will allow P3 the alley to the basket for the power slide. True, there remain two baseline defenders to stop him, but in doing so, they leave either F2 or P5 unattended. This latter play with the power slide by the high post is seen in Diagram 7-21.

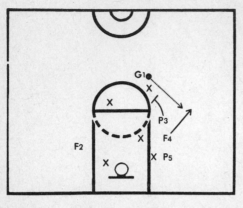

Diagram 7-20

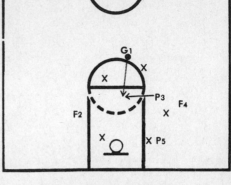

Diagram 7-21

Similarly in Diagram 7-22, G1 may force the defensive guard on the strong side to take him. P3 slides across the key, taking the middle man with him. F4 steps to the outside. P5 must now merely get in front of the nearest baseline defender to get the pass for the try at the basket. This play is the power play for the low post from Chapter 6 and it works very well. If P5 is covered, then F4 must be open. It only remains for the point guard to find the open player and pass him the ball.

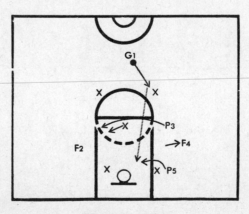

Diagram 7-22

It must be remembered that in all of these options F2 is the weak-side player. Should any play be blocked on the strong side, the ball should be reversed to the waiting F2 on the weak side. F2 needs only to stay in the seam between two defenders and try to keep an open avenue to the ball or to G1 at the point.

When the ball is reversed, as in Diagram 7-23, the posts are behind the defense and free to slash toward the ball. It works well for continuity and for success of the offense if the posts cross to their new positions with each reversal, as indicated in the diagram.

This chapter completes the general discussion of the triple stack offense. It is a unique offense with many unexplored possibilities. I am sure that you will continue to find new applications of the offense and new ways to combine it with other offenses presented in this book or with favorite offenses of your own. The next chapter contains drills for the easy and successful teaching of the triple stack offense.

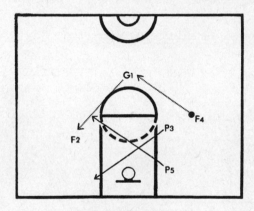

Diagram 7-23

8

Coaching
the Triple Stack
with Drills

The triple stack offense is really a combination of two offenses: the shuffle and the triple stack. If the defense cheats or tries to anticipate one, the other offense should be immediately employed to counter.

Because the drills for the coaching of the shuffle offense were discussed and illustrated in Chapter 4, they will not be repeated here, except for the drill for the basic shuffle cut. This drill is repeated because the shuffle cut occurs in the triple stack offense independent of the shuffle offense. It occurs as a back-door move by the strong-side forward from the primary formation when the ball is still at the point, and it should be drilled separately from the regular shuffle cut.

The triple stack portion of the offense is readily taught from drills presented in this chapter. Because of the simple directness of the offense and its potency, the triple stack's drills are nearly replications of the offense. The offense only uses certain moves from the primary formation and only certain other moves from the secondary formation. Because of this, the drills that teach these moves are practiced only from specific spots on the court. Consequently, they have great relevance to the offense and significant carry-over value as coaching aids.

When to Use the Drills

The drills for coaching the triple stack offense should be used from the beginning of the season. They should be begun and mastered before the initiation of the drills for the teaching of the shufffle offense. There are a couple of reasons for this. The first of these is that the triple stack is the primary offense and needs to be learned first. The second reason is that the drills in this chapter, especially the shuffle cut drill, are very similar to those drills found in Chapter 4 that teach the initiation of the shuffle offense.

The coaching of the offenses in sequence should not present problems for the players. The triple stack offense is quickly learned through the drills presented here. Moreover, it has been our experience that the entire shuffle continuity is rarely used with the triple stack since our players usually score via the shufffle cut because of its effective counter-movement to defensive cheating against the triple stack.

The teaching of the offense in sequence may even be mandatory. Experienced coaches will agree that care must be taken so that players are not confused with too much to learn at any one time.

Drills for Passing

An ideal way to begin the season is with the passing drills of this section. Passing drills teach and emphasize passing at a time when coaches are drilling fundamentals. Passing drills teach shooting from the offensive formation, and they begin teaching the offensive pattern by the parts-to-whole method.

While these drills should be continued all year, they should precede other offensive drills. All players should participate in these drills, and the passing drills should be practiced from both sides of the floor.

Drills for Passing to the Back-Door Cutter

Diagram 8-1 illustrates the most basic of the back-door drills. Two lines of players are used: one line of guards at the top of the key and a line of forwards to one side of the foul lane, in this case, the right side of the lane. The guard brings the ball to the top of the key on the dribble. As he approaches the top of the key, his partner at the forward position initiates a cut toward the basket. G must learn to anticipate this early cut, pick up his dribble and pass to F in time for the lay-up.

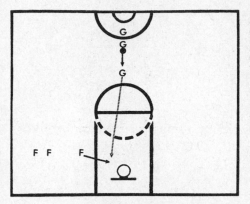 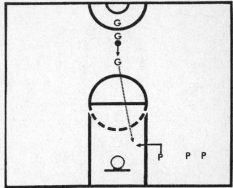

Diagram 8-1   **Diagram 8-2**

This drill simulates the initiation of the offense and the timing necessary for successful back-door passing between guard and forward. It may seem very elementary to many coaches. However, if the back-door is to be learned, it must be emphasized. After the first few days of practice, this drill may be spiced by combining it with the drill illustrated in Diagram 8-5 and by adding a defensive player to guard the forward. It then becomes a super drill that hones fine passing and cutting. It also has great defensive value for the players on defense. Remember that the triple stack operates from either side of the floor, and that this drill should be practiced from both sides of the floor.

Diagram 8-2 illustrates the drill for a necessary cut by the post. It consists of a line of guards at the top of the key and a line of posts to either side of the foul lane. The posts should take positions closer to the lane than the forwards did in Diagram 8-1. They should be right on the block-shaped hash mark.

As G approaches the top of the key, P takes a step to the inside and out toward G to clear himself of the imaginary defensive player guarding him. This is not a true back-door situation, but it prepares the players for the back-door move shown in Diagram 8-3 and simulates the move necessary for the success of the low-post power play described in Chapter 6.

Diagram 8-3 shows the back-door drill for the posts. It may be practiced with the pass from the point guard or with the pass from the

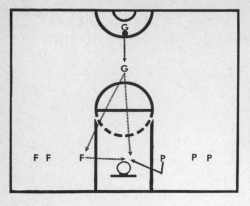

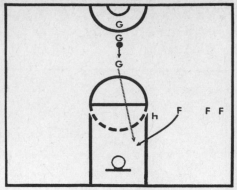

Diagram 8-3   **Diagram 8-4**

weak-side forward. Both of these passes are shown in Diagram 8-3. If
the pass comes to the post from the forward, the post will have to
delay long enough for the ball to get to the forward. The post makes
his move through a reverse pivot, a baseline cut toward the ball and
the securing of good post position on his imaginary defensive player
for the feed.

Once these two latter drills (8-2 and 8-3) have been mastered, a
defensive player should be placed on the post. The post can now
break over the top or reverse-pivot and cut behind to establish position. This drill teaches players on the perimeter to be conscious of the
interior position of the post. It also has definite defensive value for
post players.

Diagram 8-4 depicts the back-door cut to the basket by the
strong-side forward. This move will not occur very often, but it must
be practiced with regularity if the players are to take advantage of it
when it does occur. The drill is set up with a line of guards at the top
of the key and a line of forwards high and wide to one side of the key
or the other. In Diagram 8-4, the forwards are lined up to the left of
the key. A chair is used in the early season to simulate the position of
the high post. The player at the head of line F breaks to the basket to
receive a lob pass from the player at the front of line G. The pass from
G should be thrown to the outside corner of the backboard so that F
may catch it in the air and lay it in before returning to the floor. This
play will work only when the low post vacates his position. For this
reason, it is a good idea to practice this drill in conjunction with the
previous drill, Diagram 8-3. The forwards and the guards need to be
anticipating the possibility of the back-door lob.

Drills for Passing to Initiate the Offense

Diagram 8-5 illustrates the drill that teaches the pass to the weak-side forward to initiate the shuffle offense. This pass was drilled in Chapter 4. It is covered again because it needs to be drilled in conjunction with the back-door move of Diagram 8-1, especially when defense is added to the offensive forward, as suggested previously.

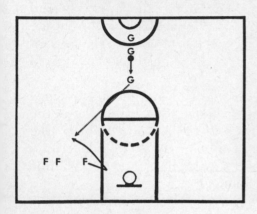
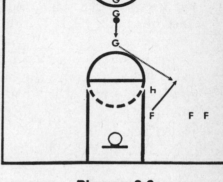

Diagram 8-5   **Diagram 8-6**

Coaching hints for this drill are as follows. First, the forward must not begin his back-door move to the basket before the guard has dribbled the ball to the top of the key. Second, his move to the basket must be a good one, and his move back outside must be made quickly by pivoting off his baseline foot. Third, the pass to the forward should be an overhead pass and must arrive when he is open. This drill must be practiced by all players and from both sides of the floor.

The simple little drill in Diagram 8-6 is very important for the forwards. It teaches them the timing necessary for the triple stack. A chair may be used in the early season, as depicted in Diagram 8-6. A forward places himself behind the chair to simulate his position in the stack. Later, of course, a post will be used so that the players can learn to adjust to real situations.

The point in Diagram 8-6 advances the ball to the top of the key, picks up his dribble and looks to the weak side away from the stack. The forward in the stack holds his position until he sees the guard pick up his dribble, and then he steps up and out of the stack. He does not make his move when the guard approaches the top of the key, as the weak-side forward does in Diagrams 8-1 and 8-5. The purpose in having the forward in the stack delay his move to the outside is to give the point guard ample time to look for the weak-side forward. The pass to the strong-side forward should be made overhead and should arrive while the forward is open if live defense is being used.

Diagram 8-7 shows a drill that is an extension of the previous drill. It is a drill that should be used once the drill shown in Diagram 8-6 is mastered. A high-post player is now added. The high post alternates receiving the pass from the point with the forward behind him. He signals when he wants the ball by holding out his outside hand (here his right hand) to call for the ball and to hold the forward behind him in the stack. This drill teaches the guard and the forward to watch for this signal.

The point guard should deliver the ball into the outstretched hand of the post player. The post should actually be turning to the outside at the time that he receives the ball so that he may take maximum advantage of the screen afforded by the strong-side forward who has held his position. The post should shoot the ball while the forward releases to rebound and follow.

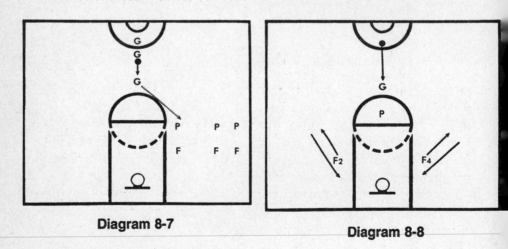

Diagram 8-7   Diagram 8-8

A Drill for Timing

Once the previous drill has been practiced to your satisfaction, the drill seen in Diagram 8-8 is helpful to insure the timing necessary for the success of the offense. G enters the ball on the dribble from the point position as before. F2 cuts back door and G can pass to F2.

If not, F2 returns outside. In the meantime, F4 has stepped to the outside from his position in the stack, using the moment that G ceased his dribble as his cue.

This drill is very helpful if G, F2 and F4 have defensive players guarding them. G must now locate the open target while facing heavy pressure himself. G must learn to use P, the high post, as a safety valve to pass to if he can find no one open. After a bit of practice, place a defensive player on P. P can now mix up his signals a bit and can vary the offensive set from primary to secondary while calling for the ball himself.

This drill is good to use all season long. It combines the major elements of the initial offense and the necessary passing requirements so that it serves as a good review that is quick and easy to run.

Drills for the Give-and-Go

Now that the previous passing drills have been learned and practiced, the give-and-go drills need to be inserted in the practice program. They are especially helpful after the point guard has learned to check off by passing to the post should the point guard not be able to find anyone else open.

Diagram 8-9

Drilling the Guard-Post Give-and-Go

Diagram 8-9 illustrates the point guard passing to the high post and then breaking to the basket for the return pass from the post. It is a good idea for the offense to use the check-off pass to the post as a signal for an automatic give-and-go attempt by the guard. The center should be reasonably open because both forwards have cleared to the outside for a pass from the point.

The pass to the post may need to be a bounce pass. Players need to understand that the give-and-go is to be attempted only on the check-off pass. No give-and-go should be attempted if the post calls for the ball by holding out his hand, indicating the power play.

Drilling the Guard-Forward Give-and-Go

Players at the point guard position need to be alerted and coached to watch for the moment that their defensive player turns his head to watch the forward with the ball. The point guard should immediately try a back-door cut behind the defensive player.

Once the point guard faces a defensive player, he should be coached to exploit this defensive tendency. This give-and-go can be practiced by putting a defensive player on the point guard during the drills illustrated in Diagrams 8-5, 8-6 and 8-9.

Screening Drills

As mentioned before, one of the distinct advantages of the triple stack is that it is so readily taught from drills. Since there are only two screens in the offense and since these occur from only two specific places on the court, putting them into beneficial drills is easy.

Drilling the High Screen

Diagram 8-10 illustrates the only drill necessary for teaching the high screen. Since this screen can only come on this side of the floor and from the primary formation, it is possible to get very specialized with regard to who practices this drill. Only point guards, high posts, and good-shooting strong-side forwards are encouraged to practice this drill. This thinking may vary from coach to coach, however, and some coaches may prefer to include all players in this drill.

As seen in Diagram 8-10, G advances the ball to the head of the key on the dribble, picks up the ball, and passes to the strong-side forward who has stepped out of the stack. Once the forward has the ball, the high post, P, steps out to screen for him. The post drives off the screen looking for the jump shot or for the post rolling to the basket. The drive by the forward will usually be over the top along the free-throw line, because the defensive player guarding the forward will trail him out of the stack, because he cannot get outside in time to deflect the pass. This delay gives the high post a very good screening angle for the drive by a right-handed forward. A good screen produces the inevitable switch by the defense. Consequently, the pass to the post should be a lob to take advantage of the mismatch.

If the defensive players switch too early, the forward should cut back or crossover-dribble and go to his left. This may get him the jump shot, but more importantly, it should get the high post on the inside of his man for the roll to the basket.

Diagram 8-10   **Diagram 8-11**

Drilling the Low Screen

Diagram 8-11 depicts the only drill necessary for teaching the low screen. Since the low screen can only come from this side of the floor and from the secondary formation, it may only be necessary to drill the players who will be playing: the point guard, the weak-side forward and both posts. Both posts should be drilled because either one may end up in the low-post position in the secondary formation. P3, the normal high post could become low post if the primary formation had been used, failed to score and, through continuity, recycled itself into the secondary formation. Refer to the triple stack continuity found in Chapter 5.

For purposes of drill and illustration, it is helpful to keep F2 in an outside position rather than have him break out to receive a pass from the point as he would in game situations. G advances the ball, picks it up and passes to F2, using the overhead pass. It now becomes necessary to coach P3 to keep his defensive player behind him as he slides toward the baseline for the pass from F2. F2 should use the bounce pass here for two reasons. First, the defensive post will have difficulty batting a low pass away when he is behind P3. Second, the player guarding F2 will normally have his hands up to prevent the pass from going inside to the low post.

Once P3 secures the ball, he continues toward the baseline with a right-handed dribble. He looks for the jump shot as he comes off a low screen by the low post, P5. If P3 was able to keep his defensive player behind him during his slide to the ball, then that defensive player should be in a very good position to be screened by P5. If the switch occurs so that P3 cannot get the jump shot, P3 should continue his dribble to the endline and lean out of bounds, that is, over the endline, for the bounce pass to the rolling P5.

Drilling Post Play

The next four illustrations show good opportunities for the posts to practice necessary one-on-one moves for their success in the offense.

As mentioned before, the posts need to practice their shooting from their positions in the power offense. The high post needs to practice jump shooting over the stack as seen in Diagram 8-12. The stack may be simulated by a chair during shooting practice.

The high post also needs to learn how to slide in front of his defensive player as in Diagram 8-13, get the pass from the point and reverse-pivot quickly for the jump shot. Both of the high post moves shown in Diagrams 8-12 and 8-13 should be practiced from both sides of the floor.

Both posts need to spend much time working on post play from the low-post positions on either side of the floor. Drills similar to those found in Diagrams 8-2 and 8-3. Other similar drills that are very good are found in Diagrams 4-17 and 4-18.

Rebounding Drills

One of the advantages of the triple stack is that its rebounding is easy to teach because the players have good position and because the shots that come from the offense are easy to anticipate. We spend quite a bit of time early in the season with a drill similar to that of Diagram 8-14. From the primary formation, you (the coach) who are indicated by C in the diagram shoot the ball and the players react by assuming rebound positions before the ball hits the basket. Using the rebounding rules set down in Chapter 5, G is the safety, F2 rebounds the weak side, P5 rebounds the strong side, P3 rebounds the short middle, and F4 rebounds the long middle.

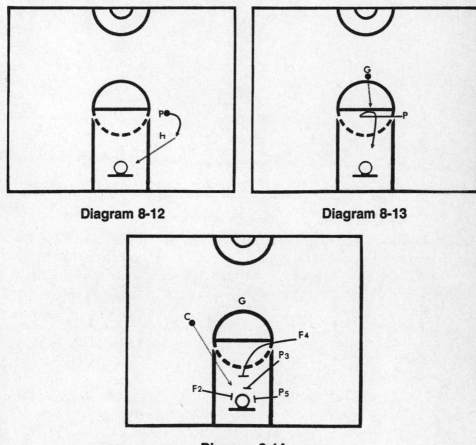

Diagram 8-12   **Diagram 8-13**

Diagram 8-14

Once the players have learned to find these positions quickly, they should be shifted into the secondary formation and apply the same rules. Next, they should be faced with defensive players and try to get to their respective spots before the ball hits the rim, while the defense trys to deny them any position at all.

From this point on, the players must learn to anticipate shots from the offense. A good method for learning this is to practice the offense without defense, and when a shot is taken, all of the players must move to rebound position before the ball hits the rim. Finally, add defensive players to the offensive practice and insist that the offense get rebound position.

Since most of the shots come from the strong side and since most missed shots will be rebounded on the side opposite, much practice is needed for the weak-side rebounders.

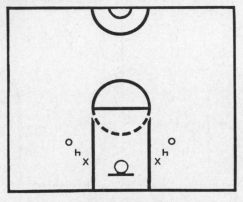

Diagram 8-15

Diagram 8-15 illustrates a drill that we put in the form of a game to help teach weak-side rebounding. The squad is divided into groups of two, and a chair is placed between the two players of each group some twelve feet from the basket. The outside player becomes the offensive player and gets the ball. The offensive player of each group must shoot the ball from behind the chair. A made basket counts two points. The defense should harass the offense but must remain behind the chair. In this way, the chair simulates a screen. Any rebound, including that of the made basket, is also worth two points. This rebounding of made baskets encourages the defense to work, and it helps the running game by teaching them to get to the ball quickly after a made basket. The players exchange positions after each shot, regardless of who got the rebound or whether the shot was made or not. A game consists of twenty points.

This chapter concludes the section on the unique triple stack offense. It also paves the way for the section on the 1-4 offense, which can be used as a pattern offense in conjunction with the triple stack or as a free-lance offense in conjunction with the passing game of the last section.

PART III

THE 1-4 OFFENSE

9

Coaching the 1-4 Offense

Perhaps no offense worries coaches of teams who play aggressive man-to-man defense more than the 1-4. Teams facing the 1-4 offense are presented with a dilemma immediately. They must either leave the basket unprotected or relinquish some of their aggressive pressure and allow the offense to set itself.

Moreover, it provides for vicious, but effective, post play. Its use of the double post forces the defense to wait until the offense is started before being able to discern the ball side from the weak side. This is a simple principle, but it swings the advantage to the offense. A defense that cannot cheat must react. It may be dictated to, rather than dictate to the offense itself.

The double post also provides for a balanced attack. While it is flip to say that basketball is not an equal opportunity sport, meaning that players must learn to fill certain roles depending on their abilities, it is true that providing an offense that affords opportunities to players to do what they can will boost morale.

Simply put, the 1-4 offense is an unusual offense based on sound basketball thinking, and players like it. It is a recipe that many coaches are looking for.

We see the 1-4 offense used as a free-lance offense, as a pattern offense, as an offense against zones and as an alignment to disguise and initiate another offense.

Advantages and Disadvantages

Up to this point, some of the striking features of the offense have been mentioned. Here are its chief advantages:

1. The 1-4 offense is impossible to pressure to the point that the ball cannot be entered to initiate the offense. There is always an open point of initiation for penetration with a pass.
2. The 1-4 provides a good vehicle for back-cutting against defensive overplays by pressure defenses or by denial defenses.
3. The 1-4 is a viable offense against zone defenses.
4. The 1-4 does not require specialized personnel. We have seen the 1-4 successfully operated with a variety of different types and sizes of ball players. It makes good use of post position, driving wing players and the pick-and-roll. These are skills that can be developed with practice.
5. The 1-4 offense utilizes some of the basketball moves that are the most difficult to defend. It employs screening-for-the-screener, the high-post rub or the "UCLA rub," the shuffle cut and the flash post.
6. Because the offense draws the defense away from the basket, the 1-4 provides good opportunity for rebounding position by the offensive players.
7. It is not an easy defense to scout.
8. The 1-4 offense is very popular with players.

The only disadvantage of this offense is that its continuity is not as easily maintained as that of other offenses in this book. The chief reason for this is that early season success with the offense encourages players to rely on the initial phase of the offense. If and when this phase of the offense fails to produce a basket, they do not readily move into the next phases of the offense.

The Basic Formation

Diagram 9-1 illustrates the initial alignment of the offense which is, of course, the 1-4 alignment. As indicated in the diagram, 1 is the point guard, 1 and 5 are the wing players, and 3 and 4 occupy the double post positions.

From this initial alignment, the offense gets its strength as well as its name. When the ball is in the hands of the point guard, the defense is unable to prevent the ball from being entered to the players on the line that consists of 2, 3, 4 and 5. In order to adequately cover these four players so that 1 has real difficulty finding someone to throw to, the defense would have to field at least six and perhaps 8 players. This would not count the defensive player guarding the point guard.

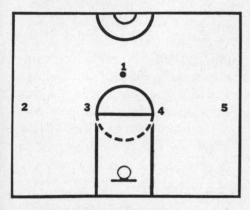 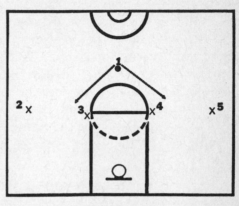

Diagram 9-1   **Diagram 9-2**

The reason that these four are so difficult to contain is that the double posts are placed high and directly in front of the point. Probably one defensive player on each of the offensive wings would be able to provide sufficient pressure to prevent the ball from being readily thrown there. However, notice the placement of 2 and 5. If the defensive players on them are playing in such a position that the ball cannot be passed directly to them, then 2 and 5 should be able to back-cut to the basket for the lob pass from the point. This is made possible by the placement of the four-in-line so far from the basket. Notice the position of the double high posts; their high position makes the back-door threat by the wings a very real possibility. Moreover, their position gives them the same back-door threat. Attempting to defense them so that the ball cannot come in directly from the point, the defense dares not front them for fear of the lob to the posts going to the basket. If on the other hand, the posts are not fronted then the pass to them must be conceded. Otherwise, the same concession must be made to the wings if the guards defending them move over to help defend the posts by virtue of a double team.

Diagram 9-2 illustrates typical man-to-man coverage of the 1-4. Playing as near the passing lane as possible and still not encouraging the back-door lob pass seems to be the rationale for such coverage. Also, covering the offense from the inside, as illustrated, leaves the outside of each post open for the pass to come in and initiate the offense. This fact of guaranteed entry is the strongest feature of the 1-4 offense.

To make the pass even easier to enter, many coaches will employ a simple maneuver as shown in Diagram 9-3. The posts are set low, and the wings drift toward the baseline as the ball is being brought to the offense. As the point guard nears the top of the key, the wings break back to the outside. At the same instant, the posts break up from the baseline. This last move is especially difficult to defense. What this maneuver does for the offense is to prevent the defense from setting up in a predetermined position, trying to anticipate the incoming pass. Some coaches will have the posts cross in the middle of the key en route to their high post positions.

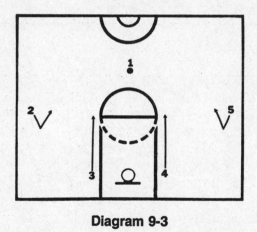

Diagram 9-3

Personnel Placement

Placement of players into this alignment is fairly standardized according to the types of positions. The post positions, 3 and 4, are usually occupied by taller, post-type players. The best passer and ball handler goes to the point position regardless of his size. If the best ball handler happens to be short, this would be the natural position for him to occupy. If he should be tall, then the offense has a real bonus when he breaks to the basket to take advantage of his height. The wing positions go to those players who would be forwards in other offenses. In filling the wing positions, look for those players who can drive a bit, and more especially, for those who play well without the ball.

If the team should have only one tall player, then look for a player who is a rugged rebounder for his size and teach him basic post play so that he might team up with the tall player at the inside positions. Tall guards will suffice instead of forwards if the team has a shortage of height, or if the guards happen to be of exceptional quality.

Keying the Offense with a Pass to the Wing

The guts of the 1-4 offense begins with the pass to the wing. This pass may go to either side as seen in Diagram 9-4. As the wings clear themselves, the pass that initiates the offense can be made.

Two things need to be noted at this point. First, any time the lob pass can be thrown to the posts or to the wings, the offense should try to score. In fact, they usually do. At that point more continuity is obviously not needed. The next chapter elaborates on the second situation where the pass cannot be made to the wings and the players defending the posts are playing directly behind the posts so that the point guard is encouraged to throw to the posts to initiate the offense.

Diagram 9-4

The main portion of the 1-4 offense, so far as this chapter is concerned, begins with the pass to wing. Which wing the point guard throws to is not really important. He merely tries to read the defense and throw to the one that is open. I try to teach my players to look for color and throw to it; this technique can be useful to the point guard.

Another factor that will determine which wing the point guard will throw to is the direction from which the defensive point guard initiates his pressure. Usually the offensive point will want to turn away from the defensive pressure and dribble into the open passing lane to shorten the pass to the wing on that side. The wing on the side that the point guard dribbles to must use this dribble as a cue to get open so that he may receive the pass.

The 1-4 Power Series

The power series is a great feature of the 1-4 offense, because it is so effective. It is effective because the offensive players are aligned high near the foul line. It is also effective because the player defending the high post will often get caught playing defense on the wrong side of the post.

Diagram 9-5 illustrates the pass to the wing on the right side of the floor and the resulting power play. Player 3 at the high post slides down the line looking for the resulting pass from 2. If 3's defender is playing on the ball side of 3, then 3 should reverse-pivot away from the defensive player and go to the opposite side of the basket for the lob pass from 2.

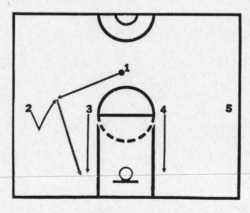

Diagram 9-5

Notice that the opposite high post goes to the basket in Diagram 9-5. This is done on cue. The posts have a rule that is standard in most types of post play involving double posts: When the ball is thrown to the other post, go to the basket.

Diagram 9-6 shows the resulting action when 3, the ball-side high post does not get the pass. He assumes a low-post position while the opposite post breaks across the key to a flash-post position. This break is a very difficult move to defend, and 4 will often get the ball from 2. Player 3 applies the post rule and immediately goes to the basket. Actually, as Diagram 9-6 shows, 3 tries to get behind his defender and come back for the ball. If he can't get the pass, then he should seal off the weak side for rebounding position.

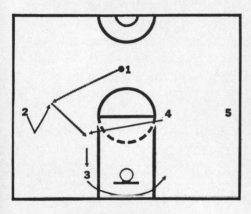
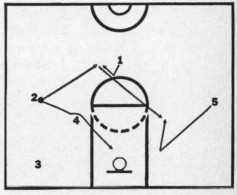

Diagram 9-6   **Diagram 9-7**

If no scoring opportunities have occurred at this point, the ball can be sent back to the point and the offense can be initiated again. The only thing that has changed in maintaining continuity is that the posts have exchanged sides. They both become flash posts eventually, as seen in Diagram 9-6. This means that when the ball is sent back to the point, they must break to the foul line extended which will open them for the pass from the point. This portion of the offense will be covered in the next chapter.

Power Play Continuity

Diagram 9-7 depicts player 2 with the ball. Player 3 slid to low post and 4 has come across the key to the flash-post position. No scoring opportunities occurred. As shown, 2 reverses the ball to 1 at the point. You will notice that this pass is the first half of the shuffle pass and that 1 clears himself in the manner described in Chapter 1.

Player 5 breaks hard at the basket and tries to create the back-door opportunity for the pass from 1. If this fails, then 5 returns to the outside for the shuffle pass from 1. Meanwhile, 2 has hesitated so that 5 had time and space to make his move. Player 2 now shuffle-cuts over 4, and the shuffle offense is under way to provide an alternate attack and continuity.

The ball has now been passed from the point to the wing, back to the point and then to the other wing. This reversal should have the defense out of position far enough so that penetration is possible. Notice the similarity to the triple stack in that the shuffle offense is closely combined with another offense. This fact may suggest other combinations and possibilities to creative coaches.

One more thing needs mentioning here. Depending upon the type of personnel that a team has, a shuffle offense suited to those players may be selected from the variety of offenses offered in Part I.

The 1-4 Rub

Teaching the 1-4 rub play also teaches a basic offensive principle: Watch the defensive play at the post. Anytime that the defensive post is playing alongside the offensive post or in front of the offensive post, the point guard should pass the ball to the wing on that side to initiate the 1-4 power play. If, however, the player defending the post is playing directly behind a high post, the point guard should begin the 1-4 rub play.

The 1-4 rub play is initiated with the pass to the wing on the same side as the post whose defender is playing from behind. It is very important that all the offensive players are aware of the position of the defensive post. If they are not, they will confound the play.

Diagram 9-8 depicts the initiation of the 1-4 rub. The point guard, 1, passes the ball to 2 at the wing. This pass is made after 1 has determined that the post is being defended from behind and after 1 has dribbled the ball into a position in front of 3 at the high post. Following the pass to 2 (who bluffed the back door in order to clear himself for the pass), 1 breaks toward the baseline and rubs his defensive player off as he passes 3 at the post. Player 2 should relay the ball to 1 as he clears the post and heads for the basket.

If the defense switches, the pass should be relayed to 3 who should go to the basket with the shorter defensive guard at his back.

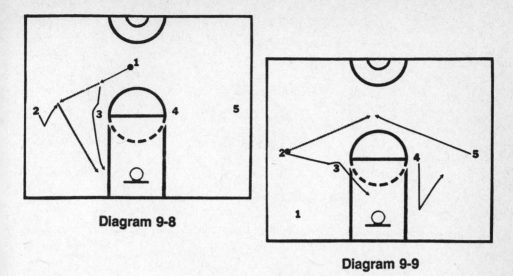

Diagram 9-8

Diagram 9-9

1-4 Rub Continuity

Following the rub past the high post, the point guard has two options if he doesn't get the ball. He can go to the corner on the ball side, or he can go to the low-post position on the opposite side of the key.

Diagram 9-9 illustrates the guard going to the corner on the side of the ball. If player 2 chooses not to pass to 1 in the corner, then his reversal of the ball to 5, filling at the point, initiates the shuffle offense. Player 4, who meanwhile broke to the low-post position, becomes the weak-side forward in the shuffle and receives a pass from 5. Player 2 shuffle-cuts off 3 at the post. The shuffle offense now maintains the continuity of the offense.

Should 2 return the ball to 1 in the corner, then any of the two-on-two or three-on-three moves depicted in Chapter 2 or Chapter 3 can be used.

Diagram 9-10 shows 1 continuing across the key to become a low post. Player 3 at the post trails and becomes a low post on the ball side; 4 flashes toward the ball. Player 2 looks for 3 and 4 as they try to secure position for the pass inside. If 2 cannot pass inside, then he reverses it to 5 at the point. Player 1 breaks to the outside for the pass, and the shuffle is underway, providing both offensive alternatives and offensive continuity.

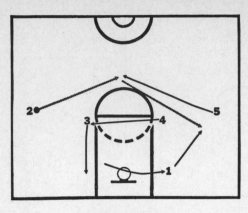

Diagram 9-10

A Word About Zone Applications

It is my experience that both the 1-4 power play and the 1-4 rub provide good offensive opportunities against zone defenses. The wings may need to be placed a couple of steps lower, initially, but the rest of the offense need not be changed.

The 1-4 alignment frustrates zones, because it distorts the zone and allows easy entry for the ball.

A coaching hint here is that the offense may break down if the shuffle is relied on to provide good shots from the perimeter. The ball should go to the post from the point whenever possible, and the post should look to the weak-side pass or for the pass to his companion post player.

Rebounding the 1-4

The 1-4 offense affords good rebounding opportunities because the defense has been drawn away from the basket. Open floor space and anticipation by the offense should produce good rebounding results.

Responsibilities for rebounding position are governed by the following rules:

1. Each post rebounds his own side of the floor.
2. The ball-side wing rebounds the middle.

This gets three rebounders in the area of the basket for offensive rebounding. If a fourth rebounder is desired offensively, the point guard should be assigned the long-middle rebounding position. In the latter case, the weak-side wing has defensive responsibilities if the opposition should suddenly get the ball.

Drills for the teaching of rebounding will be discussed in Chapter 12. The next chapter deals with the free-lance options. The 1-4 should be a free-lance offense rather than a pattern-type offense. The only pattern for the 1-4 should come from the shuffle portion of the offense.

10

Maintaining
Continuity with
Free-Lance Options

The basic 1-4 offense was described in the previous chapter along with its most popular alternative—the shuffle offense. Sophisticated defenses and careful scouting will frustrate any basic pattern offense, and the 1-4 is no exception.

The most prevalent method of defensing the basic 1-4 is to slough against it, especially against the high posts. By switching on the rub, by sloughing to prevent post play near the basket and by sloughing to deny the opportunity for the back-door cut, the defense is able to take away some of the potency of the offense. At least it takes away many of the good shots close to the basket. The defense tries to employ the same strategy as outlined in Chapters 2 and 3.

Similarly, the offensive strategy should be that of Chapters 2 and 3. The defense must not be allowed to cheat against the offense without being exploited. The only way that the defense can really cheat and be sure that they will guess what the offense will do next is for the offense to rely on patterns and pattern offense.

If the offense abandons the pattern style of play in favor of a rule-oriented continuity offense, the defense can no longer be sure that they will be able to rely on guesswork.

The advantage of free-lance offense, then, is to keep the defense off-balance and enhance offensive opportunity and continuity. Hence the title for this chapter and the suggestion that other types of free-lance play found in this book can be used in lieu of the free-lance play described here.

Rules for Free-Lance Play

For purposes of explanation and coaching of the 1-4 free-lance game, the tenet of free-lance offense, "Pass and move," is expanded to three rules here:

1. Pass to the open teammate, and pass away from pressure. Since it is impossible for the defense to smother all of the offensive players, the pass should go to the teammate who is facing the least amount of pressure and to the side of that teammate opposite the defensive player.
2. For the early part of the season, screen away from the ball. Until the offense is learned this is a wise rule. It keeps the play simpler, and it encourages play without the ball because players must cut to the ball. It also cuts down on pointless dribbling.
3. After the team is comfortable with rule number two, allow them to pass and screen on the ball as well. The pick-and-roll is now an option, as is the weave. Dribble-chase is another series that works well from the 1-4 alignment.

NOTE: Any time that the free-lance portion of the offense is being used, the basic 1-4 offense described in Chapter 9 can be employed by breaking either of the posts to the basket or by breaking the point guard to the basket.

Also, the coach has the choice of using the shuffle offense to achieve continuity or he may elect to tell the players to replace themselves after each offensive cut. Both of these continuity options are discussed in this chapter.

A discussion focusing upon the practical application of these rules follows.

Pass to the Open Teammate

Since this rule was discussed at length in the previous chapter, it will not be dealt with here.

Pass and Cut to the Basket

This option and the give-and-go options were discussed in the previous chapter; they will not be covered again here.

Screen Away from the Ball

The free-lance portion of the 1-4 should begin with the pass to one side and the screen to the other side. In Diagram 10-1, the pass to either 2 or 3 on the right side of the court may result in the screen for 4 or 5 on the left side of the court.

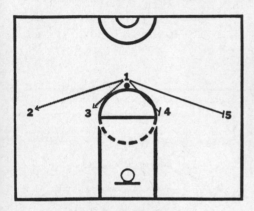

Diagram 10-1   **Diagram 10-2**

For the purpose of illustration, let us assume that the ball is first passed to the wing player, 2, as in Diagram 10-2. This pass is made to the wing only after the wing has cleared and 1 has dribbled toward that wing to shorten the passing distance and improve the passing angle.

Following the pass, 1 feints the cut at the basket before going opposite to screen for 5 at the other wing. If 1 has his man beat, he should continue to the basket. Likewise, 5, or any other player, should break back-door if he feels that he can beat his defensive player to the basket.

Meanwhile, player 4 holds his high-post position. By doing so, he creates a double screen for the breaking 5. Once 5 has cleared the screen, 4 may choose to roll through the key on a short loop, and by doing so, he becomes the second man through and is often open for the pass from 2 when 5 is not. This latter action is seen in Diagram 10-3.

Continuity

Diagram 10-3 also shows a method of maintaining continuity during the free-lance portion of the offense. You may wish to formulate this movement into a rule rather than tie it to a pattern, thereby restricting the free-lance play. The rule may state that any cutter either replaces himself or replaces a teammate who has passed and cut prior to his move.

In Diagram 10-3, player 5 replaces himself at the wing position, as does 4 if 4 does not get the ball. Player 1 returns to the point after screening since he usually doesn't need to roll to the basket when both 4 and 5 have already done so. Besides, his quick return to the point position gives 2 an open target to pass to. Once the ball is back at the point, the offense may start again.

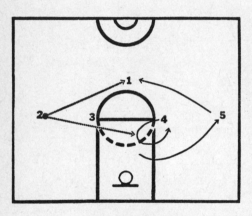

Diagram 10-3

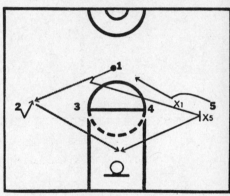

Diagram 10-4

One coaching hint needs mentioning here. If 5's defensive player leaves early to get over the screen ahead of 5, then 5 should abandon the screen and back-cut to the basket. This move is not shown. However, Diagram 10-4 illustrates another counter to defensive cheating. This diagram shows the proper reaction for a situation wherein the players guarding 1 and 5 fail to stay with their offensive players until they are able to effect a good switch. They leave their men early to exchange players by picking them up as they break into their area. Notice in the diagram that X1 and X5 hardly moved at all; X5 awaits the arrival of 1, and X1 pulls up early to wait for the expected 5. Seeing this, 1 should screen by using the two-footed jump-stop reverse-pivot immediately and then roll to the basket. Seeing this, 5

replaces 1 at the point, while 4 becomes the second man through as
before.

Diagram 10-5 illustrates the continuity for teams who like to rely
on the shuffle as the secondary offense. Player 5 remains at low post
on the ball side rather than replacing himself. Player 4 loops through
the key and breaks outside if he fails to get the ball. Player 1 breaks
back to the point after screening; player 2 passes the ball to 1. The ball
is relayed to 4, who is breaking outside. Meanwhile, 2 is shuffle-
cutting off 3 to initiate the shuffle offense. Please refer to Part I of
this book for the continuity of the shuffle that best suits your team.

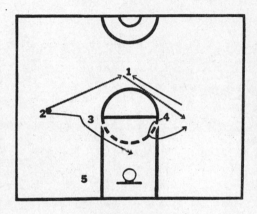

Diagram 10-5

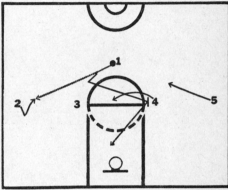

Diagram 10-6

Screening the Opposite Post

Diagram 10-6 depicts basic action for the point guard who passes
to a wing and screens for the post on the opposite side of the floor.
Generally, the play is the same as the one just described. The chief
difference is that 4 gets a single screen, whereas 5 got the double
screen. Also, expect the middle to be more congested because 1's
screen is being set in the key. Consequently, 4 may be unable to get
open very much of the time. The result may have to be similar to that
illustrated in Diagram 10-5. Player 1 passes to 2 and screens for 4.
Following the screen, 1 rolls immediately to the ball side of the
basket. Player 4 breaks off the screen to the area of the foul line for
the pass from 2 and the jump shot. Player 2 can pass to either 1 or 4,
or he can pass to 5, filling at the point position. The continuity is the
same as that of Diagram 10-3 or 10-5.

Screening on the Ball

Some free-lance offenses, especially in the passing game, do not encourage on-the-ball screens. The 1-4 offense, however, provides good scoring opportunities for players who screen on the ball.

For the sake of simplicity, you may not wish to introduce this portion to the players until other phases of the offense are well learned, especially screening away from the ball. The reason for waiting to teach the screen on the ball is to help the players away from the ball learn to read the offense and play without the basketball.

Screening the Wing

Screening on the ball is only done when the ball is at the wing position. There are three reasons for this. First, the point guard does not have a good angle from which to screen the defensive post, although he has a much better angle for the screen-and-roll when the ball is at the wing. Second, the defensive post is often stationed in the key area, and there is a very real risk of violating the three-second rule. Finally, the center of the floor is often the most congested, because the post players are often bigger, slough quickly and occupy positions that have poor passing angles to the basket.

Initiating the Play

The screen on the ball at the wing is begun with a pass from the point guard to the wing. This pass is shown in Diagram 10-7. As with the rest of the offense, the point guard, 1, may have to dribble toward the wing, 2, to shorten the distance and to improve the passing angle. Following the pass to 2 at the wing, 1 follows and screens on the ball, that is, on 2's defensive player.

The Screen and Basic Option

Diagram 10-8 illustrates player 1 screening for 2, who uses the screen. Player 3 at the post holds his position, giving, in effect, a double screen to 2. This double screen will almost certainly force a switch. To take advantage of the switch, the mismatch and the good passing lane, the post is the one who should roll to the basket. Player 2 can bounce-pass or lob-pass the ball to the rolling post.

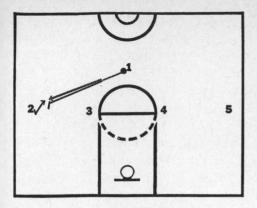

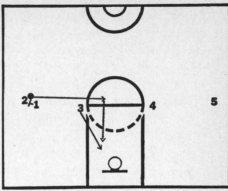

Diagram 10-7   **Diagram 10-8**

After 3 has rolled to the low-post position and if he failed to get the pass from 2, the other post player breaks toward the ball as shown in Diagram 10-9. If 4 is able to beat his defensive player to the middle of the key and get position, the pass from 2 should lead to the lay-up.

If, on the other hand, player 4's defensive player tries to deny 4 the flash-post position and fronts him coming across the key, 2 should continue to dribble until he is on the other side of 4 as pictured in Diagram 10-10. This maneuver places the defensive player guarding 4 on the wrong side and allows 4 to roll to the ball unmolested.

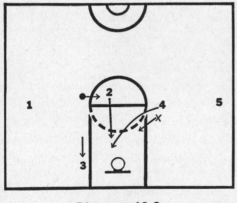

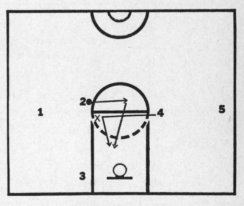

Diagram 10-9   **Diagram 10-10**

Continuity

Diagram 10-11 illustrates the continuity for this particular portion of the offense. The continuity is readily maintained from this point by using the shuffle. Player 2 has the ball at the point because he did not pass to anyone else. The opposite post, 4, has flashed to 1's side. Player 5 executes a back-door move. If that is unsuccessful, he then breaks to the outside for the shuffle pass from 2 and 1 shuffle-cuts past 4.

If a team prefers to use free-lance options entirely and not to rely on the shuffle as a means of maintaining continuity, then 3 should have posted on the opposite side. (Refer to the play depicted in Diagram 10-8.) After 4 has flashed to the opposite side of the key and 2 has dribbled to the center of the floor, then 3 may break to the high post as shown in Diagram 10-12, and the offense is ready to begin again.

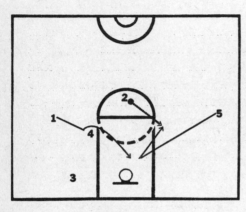

Diagram 10-11

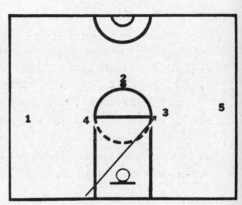

Diagram 10-12

The Cut-Back

If the defensive player guarding 2 tries to fight over the top of the screen or if he tries to slough over and guard 1 while player 1's guard waits atop the screen for 2, then 2 should execute the cut-back as exhibited in Diagram 10-13. To execute the cut-back, 2 merely begins dribbling toward the baseline. This takes him away from the cheating defender. The player guarding 1 must now switch over to 2 or watch 2 go all the way to the basket. When the defender leaves 1, 1 is free to roll to the basket as shown.

Using the Point Guard as a Post

A very nice play is shown in Diagram 10-14. When the point guard screens for 2 at the wing, he is positioned nearer the baseline than any of the other offensive players. This position makes him a post player of sorts, whose post position is made effective by moving the ball. Assume that the point guard's defender followed the point guard to his screen. If the defender tried to get into the passing lane to take away the give-and-go, then the quick pass to the post would place that defender on the wrong side of his man and allow the point guard to roll to the basket.

This play is merely another way of achieving the pass option to the pick-and-roll. It does, however, make the point guard a post. This is advantageous when the point guard has a height advantage. It is also advantageous because the defender is not apt to be accustomed to post-type defense.

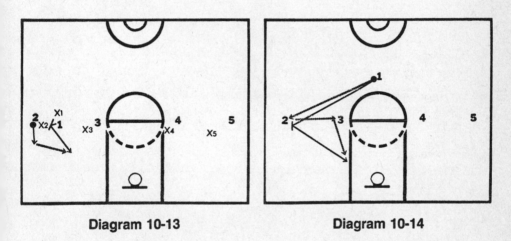

Diagram 10-13   Diagram 10-14

The Hand-Off

Another method of arriving at the screen play just described is the outside handoff. This play is especially helpful if the team uses the weave with the 1-4, which is an option to be discussed later in this chapter.

Diagram 10-15 illustrates the outside handoff. The point guard passes to the wing and follows, but instead of screening on the inside for 2, he breaks off 2 to the outside. This, in effect, makes 2 the screener and forces a defensive switch. The handoff from 2 to 1 and the switch as 1 begins to drive should allow 2 to roll to the basket. Either the lob or bounce pass can be used. By pivoting as he hands off, 2 can be sure that he sets an effective screen.

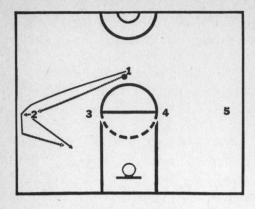

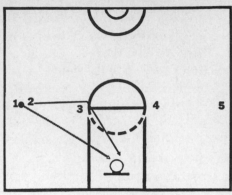

Diagram 10-15   **Diagram 10-16**

If player 1 is forced to pick up his dribble by an aggressive jump-switch, the play can be varied by cutting 2 over the post as shown in Diagram 10-16. A subsequent lob pass from 1 can score. The continuity for the handoff series is maintained by moving 5 out to the point and passing to the point either to begin the shuffle offense or to recycle the 1-4. If the latter is the case, either 1 or 2 will have to fill for 5.

Hitting the Post

As in most offenses, the point guard should try to pass to the post as often as possible. The post players, 3 and 4, should try to maintain position so that they are open to receive the pass. If a post has position and gets a pass from the point, he should attempt a one-on-one move to the basket.

If, however, that post gets a pass and is unable to make the move to the basket, then the other post should break to the basket as shown in Diagram 10-17. This is a sound principle of post play.

The point guard passes to the right post, 3, as the other post, 4, breaks over the top of his defensive player. He hopes that this move will maintain an open passing lane to 3 so that he can get the pass for a one-on-one move to the basket. It is helpful for the on-side wing, 2, to slide toward the baseline so that his defensive guard cannot interfere with the play of the posts. He may even be able to beat his defender with a quick back-door move.

The point guard, meanwhile, goes to the opposite side of the floor to screen for the other wing. This screen can pop 5 open on his "second man through" move to the basket. Any premature switching by the defense should prompt 1 to roll to the basket from his screen and secure position for the lob pass from 3.

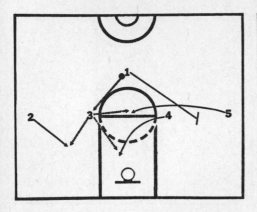

Diagram 10-17   **Diagram 10-18**

Continuity

If the pass to the post fails to produce a score or if 3 passes to 5 coming off the screen and is unable to go to the basket, the offense may then wish to go to the shuffle for continuity. Diagram 10-18 illustrates the pass from 3 to 5. Player 1 pops out from his screening position for the shuffle pass from 5, and 2 shuffle-cuts past 3 to begin. Note that 4 posted low as usual.

If the shuffle is not being used for continuity, 4 should replace himself at the post. Player 2 should fill at the point, while 5 replaces 2 for balance.

The Screen-and-Roll

Careful analysis of the offense should lead to the conclusion that the only truly effective screens-and-rolls will be initiated by the on-side post. The on-side post should be encouraged to screen for the player with the ball whenever possible in the free-lance game.

Diagram 10-19 illustrates 3 stepping out from his post position to screen for the point guard. The point guard drives off this screen and post 3 rolls to the basket for the pass. The on-side wing, 2, should drop down, away from the play, so that his guard will be unable to step over to help defend against the screen-and-roll. The shuffle continuity can be used by moving 5 to the point as shown and returning 3 to the post if he does not get the pass.

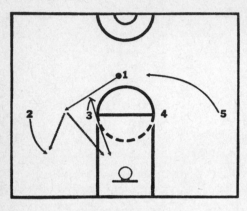

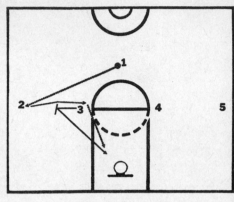

Diagram 10-19   **Diagram 10-20**

The Screen-and-Roll with the Wing

The post can effectively screen for the on-side wing as shown in Diagram 10-20. Here the point passes the ball to 2 at the wing. The high post on that side steps over to screen for the wing, who drives over the top, which should force a switch. Player 3 rolls to the basket to take advantage of the mismatch.

Continuity for this play will depend upon what player 1 did after his pass to the wing. Refer to the appropriate diagram for the continuity.

The Weave and the 1-4

By incorporating the weave into the offense as described in Chapter 3, the 1-4 becomes very difficult to defend against and it also becomes very diverse for several reasons. The weave is similar to the handoff play or option described in this chapter. It can be incorporated with the shuffle offense or used with the weave of the shuffle offense. It can also be used with the high-post passing game described in Chapter 14.

The weave has been thoroughly described in Chapter 3 and need not be repeated here. The players involved in the actual weaving are the point guard and the two wings. As the ball is moved from side to side on the dribble the posts should be free to roll to the basket anytime the defensive players get out of position. When one of the posts does roll to the basket, the other should flash-post. The post who rolled exits on the opposite side of the key and then resumes the high-post position. The wings, or the players who have the ball in the wing position, should be encouraged to look for the drive first, the post second and the shot last. The post without the ball should go to the basket when the other post has the ball.

With a bit of work this offense makes an excellent stall or slow-down game. It has some advantages that the four-corner offense doesn't have, especially the fact that the 5-second count is constantly being broken as the ball is taken past the 28-foot hash marks.

As mentioned in the previous chapter, continuity in the 1-4 offense will be difficult to maintain, especially if the offense is relied upon as presented in Chapter 9. As with the other offenses in this book, continuity of a basic offense can be enhanced through the judicious use of free-lance play. This chapter has concentrated on popular free-lance options. Chapter 11 will focus on variations of the 1-4 offense with the same goal in mind.

11

Developing
Popular
1-4 Variations

Like other offenses contained in this book, the 1-4 offense is versatile. It can be blended with other offenses or varied slightly as this chapter demonstrates. First, however, a brief discussion concerning the nature of and reasons for change.

Why Variations Were Devised and What They Do

The variations described in this chapter are the 1-4 inside offense, the 1-4 outside offense, the 1-4 swing offense, and the 1-4 baseline offense. These variations range from subtle pattern changes seen in the 1-4 inside offense and the 1-4 outside offense to the more radical changes in the 1-4 swing offense and the 1-4 baseline. Each variation has its purpose and its merits. In keeping with the theme of this book, each offense also has its own continuity.

The 1-4 inside offense is very similar to the initial option described in Chapter 10. It differs in that it looks for the post every time. The inside offense is a good offense to use if the defense is sagging away from the posts or if the wings are being overplayed by the defense. It is also a good offense to run with a good passing post who can not do other things well.

The 1-4 outside offense is very similar to the original offense. It is an effective offense to use when a team has a pair of post players who work well together or who are mobile. Also, it gains dimension when the point guard is tall or a good shooter.

The 1-4 baseline offense is made to order for the team that has a very tall post player but wants to use the 1-4. It is also the offense to use if the team has a good shooting post. This offense keeps one post low and varies the pattern quite radically from the traditional 1-4.

The 1-4 swing offense is designed for the team with a tall, mobile wing. It takes the wing to the basket and allows him to utilize his height. The 1-4 swing does not require an exceptional post. If a player can screen and rebound, then he can play post in this offense.

Since each of these offenses has different player requirements, they afford coaches a selection of 1-4 offenses that use personnel different from those required for the traditional offense as a result of the changes made.

The 1-4 Inside Offense

The 1-4 inside offense uses the standard 1-4 alignment: the point guard is out front at the top of the key, the wings are on either side of the free-throw line extended and the two posts are at the high-post positions on each side of the key.

Using the alignment seen in Diagram 11-1 the best passing post would be in the 3 position. This assumes that the post is right handed. It also assumes that 5, the off-side wing is right handed and can utilize that advantage as he comes from left to right.

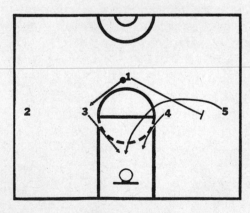

Diagram 11-1

Operational Movement

Diagram 11-1 also shows the initial stage of the offense. The point guard passes the ball to the high post, 3, if the defense is sagging away from 3 or if 3 is a good passer. For whatever reason, 3 gets the pass to initiate the offense, although the pass could have gone to 4 at the other post in which case offense is run to the other side. By passing to the inside, to the post, the offense is keyed and accordingly named "the inside offense."

Following the pass to the post, 1 bluffs the give-and-go cut to the basket to set up a good screening angle for 5. As the screen is being set (1 should use the two-footed jump-screen described in Chapter 13), 5 starts to back-cut to the basket, times his move and cuts over the top of the screen for the pass from 3. If he is successful in losing his guard, the defensive player guarding 4 will probably switch to him as he comes over the top. For this reason, 4 should roll to the basket as indicated in the diagram.

Player 1 should only roll to the basket when the defensive players make their switch prematurely. (Refer to Diagram 10-4.) Player 5 should not hesitate to use the back-cut in this offense because it affords a great passing angle with the ball at the high post. Player 2 should be alert to this situation for the same reason.

Inside Continuity

The inside 1-4 can maintain continuity through either the shuffle or free-lance offense.

The shuffle continuity for the inside offense is seen in Diagram 11-2. If 5 is not open on his move over the screen, he should pull up and become the point guard, while 1 assumes a new position at the wing. Player 3 returns the ball to 5 at the point who shuffle-passes it to 1. Meanwhile, 2 shuffle-cuts past 3. Note the position of 4, who is now the strong-side forward in the shuffle offense.

If the wing, 5, cuts through the key instead of filling the point position, 1 should replace himself at the point. Player 5 should exit the key and resume his position at the wing in time for the shuffle pass.

From this point on, after initiation of the shuffle offense, the shuffle becomes the primary offense and utilizes the shuffle continuity of Chapters 1 and 2.

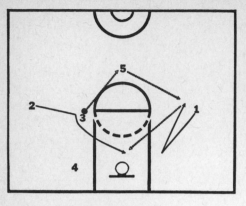

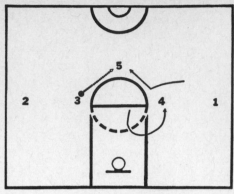

Diagram 11-2   **Diagram 11-3**

Diagram 11-3 illustrates one method of maintaining continuity by recycling the offense. If 5 doesn't get the ball, he takes the point position. Player 1 takes the wing position, and 4 replaces himself. The ball is returned to 5 at the point, and from this point on the offense can repeat the inside 1-4 by passing to one of the posts, initiating the free-lance play described in the last chapter or adopting one of the other offenses in this chapter.

The 1-4 Outside Offense

Like the 1-4 inside, the 1-4 outside utilizes the traditional alignment.

The good-shooting guard takes the point position in this offense. The best ball-handling post or the best shooting post takes the 4 position.

Operational Movement

Diagram 11-4 illustrates the basic pattern for the 1-4 outside offense. As with other 1-4 offenses, the wings bluff the back-door move to clear themselves, and the point guard dribbles toward one of them (here player 2) to shorten the passing distance and to improve the passing angle. The point guard, 1, passes the ball to player 2 at the wing. Following the pass, 1 and 3 rub at the corner of the free-throw lane. Should 1 get open, 2 passes the ball to him for the subsequent lay-up. If 1 does not get the pass, he goes to the corner below the ball. Meanwhile, 3 continues across the key to screen for 4.

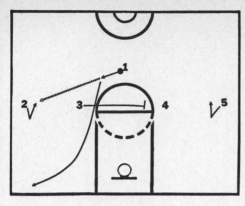
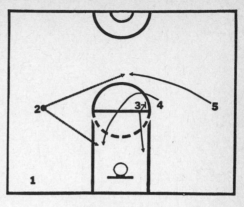

Diagram 11-4   **Diagram 11-5**

Diagram 11-5 shows a continuation of this play. Player 3 is seen screening for 4, who cuts over the screen for the pass and the possible lay-up. Players 3 and 4 must work together to maximize the number of scoring options. Player 4 should bluff the move to the basket to occupy his defensive guard's attention so that 3 is able to get a good angle on the guard. If the switch occurs, 3 should roll to the basket. If the defensive players "exchange men," that is, if they do not stay with their assigned players until the screen is set but wait for their new assignment coming out of the screen, then 3 should bluff the screen and cut immediately to the basket.

Meanwhile, player 5 fills the point position vacated by 1. Player 5 should always feel free to back-door his opponent if possible or to break over the top of 3's screen as the second man through. If he does either one of these things and fails to get the ball, then 2 should dribble the ball out to the point, 1 should fill up for 2 and 5 should replace 1. (Diagram 11-6)

Before moving the ball to the point, either by pass or dribble, 2 should look for 1 in the corner. Remember that 1 should be the good-shooting guard, and if his defensive player sloughs toward the middle to help defend the posts, then 1 may be open for the good shot.

Continuity

Continuity for the 1-4 outside offense is the shuffle. Because of the alignment of the offensive players following the operational movement, the shuffle is the logical method for maintaining continuity.

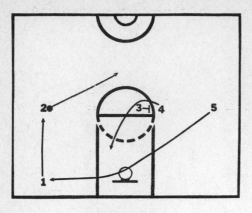

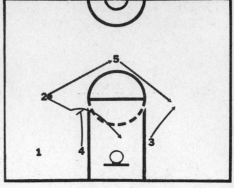

Diagram 11-6   **Diagram 11-7**

In Diagram 11-7, player 2 has the ball since he received the pass. He can easily pass to 5, filling in at the point, to initiate the shuffle offense. Player 5 looks for 3 coming back outside after he rolls to the basket, and 4 moves up to screen for the shuffle-cutting 2. The shuffle offense is continued until a shot is made.

The 1-4 Swing Offense

For the team with the tall quick player, who fits the forward mold more than the post mold, the 1-4 swing offense is worth considering. This offense has more merit if the post players are average. You may feel that with such personnel the 1-4 type offense should be scrapped in favor of another type of offense. However, if you like the 1-4 and if you have the personnel mentioned above, the swing offense provides some solutions. The 1-4 swing can be combined with other 1-4 offenses or with an offense that is entirely different to best suit the given personnel.

Operational Movement

The 1-4 swing operates from the traditional 1-4 alignment as shown in Diagram 11-8. Assuming that 5 is the tall mobile forward, the pass signaling the start of the offense should be made away from him. To decoy this move, however, both wing men bluff a cut to the basket and come outside for the ball. The point guard dribbles at 2 to insure a good pass and then passes to 2. Posts 3 and 4 drop into a tandem position to double screen for 5 coming underneath. Player 2 relays the ball to 5 as soon as 5 is able to get open. If the defense switches, then 3 rolls to the ball. Player 4 would roll if 5 goes over the top of the double screen and if the defense switches.

Like all 1-4 offenses, the swing can be run to either side of the floor, but it should be run to the side where the pass can be made most easily.

Continuity

Diagram 11-8 illustrates the basic continuity for the 1-4 swing. If 2 is unable to get the pass to 5 as he comes past the screen, he should hold the ball for an additional second to give 5 a chance to post up. Player 2 should also be alert to the possibility of the roll by either 3 or 4.

If none of these options materialize, however, then 2 passes the ball back out to the point. This pass keys another double screen by the posts for 5, who swings back across the key as seen in Diagram 11-9. Another pass from 2 to 1 would signal yet another double screen and cut by 5.

This continuity can be easily varied by switching to the tandem shuffle explained in Chapter 2. Also, note the similarity of this offensive alignment to that of the triple stack. It would be easy to convert to the triple stack offense as well.

Diagram 11-8

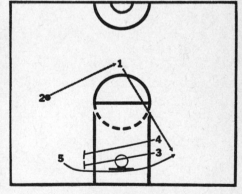

Diagram 11-9

A Swing Option

In Diagram 11-10, player 5 brings the ball to the point. He is free to pass the ball to either wing. For the sake of illustration, he passes to 1. The posts set the double screen a bit higher and to the same side of the floor that the pass went. In this case the screen is to the left side. Next, 5 swings through the key and around the double screen as shown. Player 1 gives him the ball as shown.

If 5 is not open, 1 returns the ball to 2 who has rotated to the point. Player 5 swings under the double screen again for the pass from 1. From this point on, the continuity is similar to that of the standard 1-4 swing offense, the triple stack, or the tandem shuffle. (Diagram 11-11)

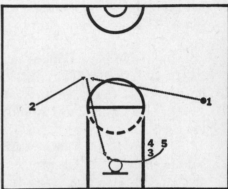

Diagram 11-10   **Diagram 11-11**

The 1-4 Baseline Offense

The 1-4 baseline offense is a post-oriented offense that can be easily blended with the standard 1-4 or with the 1-4 swing. It operates from the standard 1-4 set.

Operational Movement

Diagram 11-12 shows the initial alignment and the beginnings of the offense. As in the standard 1-4 operation, the wings move toward the basket and then come back out for the pass from the point guard who has dribbled toward his target. Player 1 passes to 2, and 3 and 4 both make post moves toward the basket. If 2 is able to hit 3, then 3 should be in position to take his defensive player to the basket. If he can't hit 3, he should look for the other post who is already going to the basket.

If 2 is unable to get the ball to 3, then 3 posts up and allows 4 to rub his defensive guard off en route to the ball as pictured. Meanwhile, 5 takes a weak-side rebounding position.

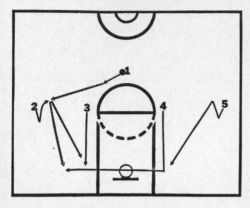 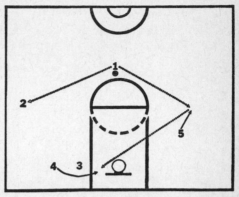

Diagram 11-12   **Diagram 11-13**

Continuity

Diagram 11-13 illustrates the configuration of the offense following the previous move of the offense. From this point, the ball can be reversed to the point to 5 as he pops out at the wing, and the shuffle can be initiated as in previous 1-4 offenses.

A variation in the continuity is shown in 11-13. Once the ball has been reversed around the horn, 4 can try to rub his guard off on 3 by cutting to the ball. If he fails to get the ball, he posts up while 3 trails, executes a rub on 4 and looks for the pass from 5. Player 5 looks for either 4 on the post-up move or 3 as he comes around 4. (Diagram 11-14)

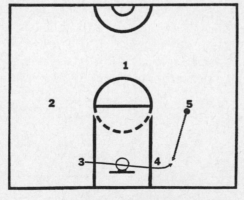

Diagram 11-14

Split-the-Post Options

An alternate form of continuity can be obtained by splitting the post. Diagram 11-15 resumes the action shown in Diagram 11-12. Player 2 still has the ball and feeds into the post. He follows his pass and splits the post with 4. If 1 is a good jump shooter, a three-man split can be used involving player 1.

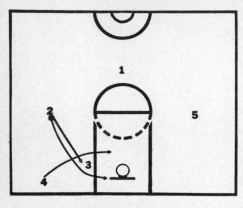
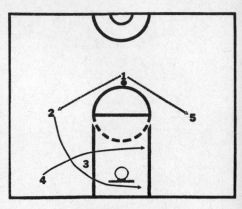

Diagram 11-15   **Diagram 11-16**

A variation of this split is seen in Diagram 11-16. The ball is reversed around-the-horn to 5, while 2 and 4 execute the scissors around 3. Player 3 can trail these two and post up for a hit-and-split similar to that of 11-15 or the ball can be reversed and the post split again.

This concludes the discussion of the popular variations of the 1-4. As with the standard 1-4 offense, the shuffle, the triple stack and the passing game, these variations have a continuity that relies on reversing the ball to distort the defense so the defense becomes more vulnerable than if it was allowed to remain in an initial set.

The next chapter presents drills for the coaching and implementation of the 1-4 offense, its options and its variations.

12

Coaching
the 1-4
with Drills

The 1-4 offense is readily broken down for teaching by the parts-to-whole method. This chapter details drills for entering the ball with the pass, cutting through the offense to get the ball, screening, interior post play and rebounding.

The drills in each of these areas are sequential insofar as the individual area is concerned. The progression through the drills need not depend upon mastery of an entire set of drills before another set of drills is attempted. Rather, drills of several phases of the game may be initiated at the same point in the season.

An efficient method of coaching the drills, if coaching personnel permits, is the simultaneous drill of outside personnel and inside personnel. This is done by having the post players drill on post moves at one end of the court, while guards and wing men drill at the other. Drills that require both posts and outside people, of course, must be practiced by the entire team.

1-4 Passing Drills

Passing drills for the coaching of guard-to-wing or guard-to-post passes are included in this section. These passes are important because they initiate the offense and key what happens next. The passes need to be made correctly to protect possession of the ball while penetrating the defense.

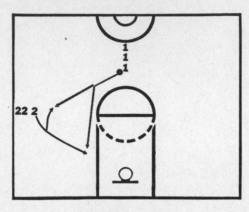

Diagram 12-1

The Pass to the Wing

Diagram 12-1 illustrates the coordination of efforts by the point guard with the ball and one of the wings. This drill needs to be practiced on both sides of the floor by all of the outside people.

In 12-1, the point guard, 1, signals that he is about to initiate the offense on the right side of the floor by dribbling right. This dribble to the right also shortens the passing distance to the wing. He should dribble to a position just outside the foul circle. As he does this, 2 initiates a move to the basket and 1 passes the ball to 2 for the back-door lay-up as shown. From this same drill, 2 can practice beginning the back-door cut returning to the outside for the pass from 1.

Coaching hints for the cutter, 2, are as follows. When 2 starts to the basket, the move should be done with instant acceleration. He should either try to get between the imagined defensive player and the ball for the race to the basket or he should reverse-pivot to get his imagined defensive player on his back and accelerate to the basket. The comeback should be made by planting the outside foot, pivoting on that foot and pushing off with that same foot to come back to the ball. This move will insure that a defender, real or imagined, will be on the backside of the cutter and unable to disrupt the pass.

The pass itself needs special attention. Some proponents of the 1-4 maintain that the pass from the point should be made off the dribble; the dribbler should never pick up his dribble. This method has merits, however, it is not in keeping with the theme of this book; all of the offenses in this book can be blended together or used in varied forms. Also, I contend that the pass from the dribble is a highly specialized kind of pass that has many risks attached. Instead, a pass similar to the shuffle pass described in Chapter 1 is recommended. The point guard picks up his dribble, lifts the ball overhead and pivots to face the basket. The pass may now be made overhead, especially if 2 is going all the way to the bucket, or it can be passed off the defender's hip as a bounce pass if the defender has his arms extended to discourage the overhead pass.

The Pass to the Post

Diagram 12-2 shows the pass from the point to the post. As before, this drill should be practiced to both sides of the floor. It should be practiced by all guards and post players.

The player at the head of the line of guards initiates by dribbling to the outside of the foul circle as he did in the previous drill. He picks up his dribble and pivots as he did before. This time, however he passes to 3 at the post.

While correct execution by 1 must be insisted upon, 3 must get his share of the attention. It is 3, after all, who makes the offense so versatile because of his high-post position. He must learn to use it to advantage beyond clearing the floor for the back-door move by the wing.

Diagram 12-2

He must learn to control the offense. The following hints are recommended. If his imagined defensive player is defending from the inside, 3 should set up a step closer to the inside. This gives him an additional step on the ball side with which to work. If the defender sets on his outside, he would move a step to the outside for the same reason.

As 1 nears the spot where he will pick up his dribble, 3 must execute a partial pivot against his defensive player to get the defender on his backside, make contact and try to hold that position without violating the 3-second rule. Once he has done this, he gives the point guard a target by holding out the hand away from the defender. He must help the point guard read the defense. If the guard's defender has his hand or hands down, the target is given high; if the guard's defender has his hands high, then the target is given low to call for the bounce pass. There is no danger of ball loss in the bounce pass because the tall defender at the post is unable to reach and stoop enough to deflect the low incoming pass if the pass is made to the open side of 3.

Diagram 12-2 shows 3 pivoting to control his defender. If the defender fronts, then the lob pass to the rolling 3 should be practiced. This drill assumes that the defender, real or imagined, does not play defense from behind.

After 1 and 3 have made their play, 3 drives to the basket for the lay-up, and each returns to the end of their respective lines while the next pair takes a turn.

This drill can be made progressively more difficult by adding defense; first dummy, then live.

Drills for the Cutter

The drills for the cutter are logical three-man extensions of the two-man passing drills. Like the passing drills, they should be executed on both sides of the court. In each of these drills, a line of guards, a line of wings and a line of posts is needed. Players return to their respective lines following their participation in the drill.

Cutting the Wing

Diagram 12-3 illustrates the pass from the point to the post and the relay to the cutting wing. This play is a drill that teaches the proper reaction to the situation wherein the pass can not be made to the wing because of intense overplay by the wing's defender. Notice in the diagram that the wing tries to back-door, comes back for the pass and finally succeeds in getting open by the cut to the basket.

It is 3, however, who makes the play work, he controls his defender so that the pass to him can be made. His passing lane to 2 is also better than that of 1.

All of the previous points of emphasis apply. Added to them is the recommendation that 3 have his legs under him before passing to 2. The type of pass he uses can vary.

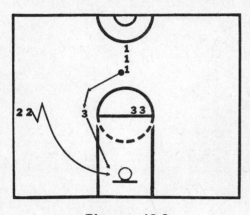

Diagram 12-3   **Diagram 12-4**

Cutting the Post

Diagram 12-4 depicts the companion play to 12-3. Here, the pass can not be made to the post because of successful overplay by the imaginary defense. The wing was able to get the pass, however, and relay it to the cutting 3. Player 3 is now able to use the defensive overplay to advantage as he locks the defender to the outside with a reverse pivot and rolls to the basket.

All of the previous points of emphasis apply.

The Rub

As mentioned in Chapter 9, the rub becomes automatic when the defender plays behind the post, thus conceding the pass.

In such cases, the post should remain as high as possible to allow the cutting guard room to work. As pictured in Diagram 12-5 the pass goes to the wing, and the point tries to rub off his guard en route to the basket. It is important that 3 remains stationary so that 1 can set up the defense. Player 1 does this by maneuvering his defender at 3/4 speed until he feels that he has the defender at a disadvantage, whereupon he accelerates to the basket. After live defense has been added to this drill, 3 will want to roll to the basket if a defensive switch occurs. Defense should be added to each of the last three drills as soon as players have mastered the execution of the fundamentals.

Diagram 12-5

Drills for the 1-4 Double Post

You will want to drill your post players on basic interior post play when teaching the 1-4. These next six drills are for the posts and need not involve other players, but they should be practiced from both sides of the floor.

The Power-Slide

Diagram 12-6 illustrates the coaching of the power-slide. You assume the role of the wing, while the post executes a reverse pivot, slides down the outside of the key, takes a pass from you and powers to the basket. Besides correct pivoting, giving the target and protecting the ball during the slide will need emphasis.

This is a good drill for learning to make the most of incoming passes. You may want to throw poor passes intentionally, to emphasize the importance of retrieving the ball and to improve agility.

The Slide and Reverse

The drill in Diagram 12-7 is a logical extension of Diagram 12-6. Should 3 be unable to get the pass on the power-slide, he should continue to the low-post position as shown. Next, he posts up, gets position for the pass and reverse-pivots into the key for the hook or short jumper. You should insist that proper post position and a hand target to call for the ball are used by the post before the pass is thrown.

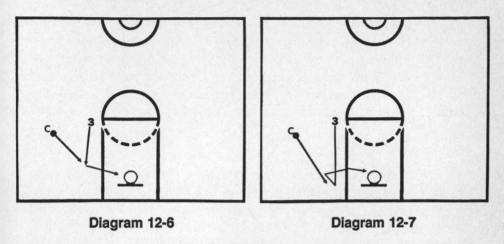

Diagram 12-6   Diagram 12-7

The Flash Post

Diagrams 12-8 and 12-9 begin a series of drills for the posts from the high positions. The first of these shows moves for the post opposite the ball as he flashes to a post position on the ball side.

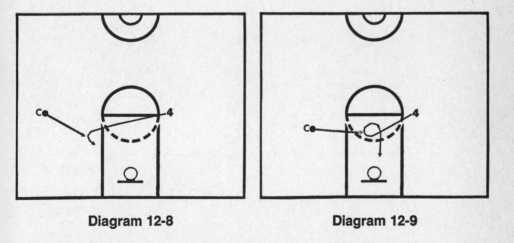

Diagram 12-8   Diagram 12-9

Diagram 12-8 shows the pass to the post as he arrives at his new position, subsequently pivots and either power-slides to the basket or executes a turn-around jumper.

Diagram 12-9 illustrates the pass to the post as he approaches his new position, the reverse pivot and the jump shot or lay-up.

Both of these moves require that the flash post control his defender once he has arrived at the flash position. Ideally, the post would like to be able to control the defense during the break to the new position, but this will not always be possible. Insist on quick moves to the ball and control of the area once there. Good defensive teams will have the defensive post player fight the offensive player as he comes across the key. The next drill teaches moves that will soften this defensive pressure and help the flash post in future cuts.

The Post-to-Post Pass

In the 1-4, as in other offenses, it is wise to release one post to go to the basket when the other post has the ball. Diagram 12-10 depicts the ball coming in from your pass from the point. Player 3 controls his defensive player so that he is able to get the pass. Once the pass is securely in his possession, he pivots to face the basket while the other post makes his move. The other post can break over the top of his guard, or he can reverse-pivot and go to the basket for the lob.

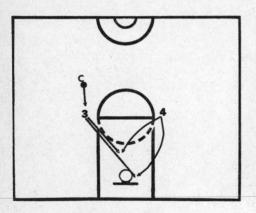

Diagram 12-10   **Diagram 12-11**

The Post-to-Post Screen

Diagram 12-11 depicts the last of the post drills. In this drill, one post screens for the other to break to the ball. You have the ball at the wing position while 3 goes across to screen for 4. Good screening technique should be emphasized. Player 3 should use the two-footed jump-screen, and 4 should leave to go over the top of the screen at the precise instant that 3 alights.

Beyond this, 3 should be coached to roll immediately. The reason for this is that the defensive posts will slough and switch against this move so that 3 will be open on the deep roll to the basket.

As with all of the post drills in this section, this drill should be practiced from both sides of the floor. Live defense should be added as moves are mastered.

Screening Drills

The next section of drills to be discussed is the section on screening. These drills are to be practiced from both sides of the floor by all the players. The first of these are the off-ball screens.

Screening for the Post

This drill can be taught as a continuation of the drills in Diagrams 12-4 and 12-5. The only difference is that the post is on the opposite side of the floor. You may wish to cover or drill the give-and-go aspects of this drill before beginning.

The action is seen in Diagram 12-12. The point guard moves the ball from the head of his line to a position outside the foul circle. The player at the head of line 2 becomes the wing, moves to get open, receives the pass and pivots to face the action. Player 1 bluffs the give-and-go (he may go all the way) to set up the good screening angle for the screen on the post, 4. Player 1 screens 4, 4 breaks over the

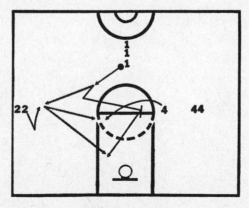

Diagram 12-12

screen and 1 rolls to the basket. Player 2 may pass to either 1 or 4. All fundamental methods and techniques taught in the previous drills should be emphasized and executed.

After the play, the players go to the ends of their respective lines, the next trio repeats the drill and so on. Once mastered, this drill should be practiced with live defense.

Screening for the Wing

The drill in Diagram 12-13 is identical to that of the previous drill except that a wing player has been added at 5. Following his pass to 2, 1 screens for 5. Player 5 cuts over the top of the double screens and 4 follows as the second man through.

This drill should be practiced from both sides with all previous fundamentals emphasized.

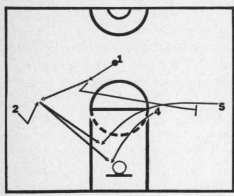
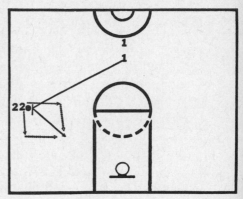

Diagram 12-13   **Diagram 12-14**

Screening on the Ball

Diagram 12-14 shows two lines, one at the point and one at the wing. To begin this drill, the ball is placed in the hands of the player at the head of line 2 in the wing position. Player 1, at the head of his line, moves over to screen for 2. Once the screen is set, 2 may choose to use it or not, depending on what the defense does. If 2 is able to execute a good drive off the top of the screen and loses his guard, he can drive to the bucket. He must be ready, however, to pass to 1 on the roll to the basket if the defense switches. If the defense on 2 tries to cheat over the top of the screen, then 2 will want to back-cut and dribble toward the baseline. Again, he looks for the rolling 1.

Points of emphasis are as follows: Player 1 must move into the screen quickly but under control. He uses the two-footed jump-screen mentioned previously. Player 2 must time his move to coincide with that of player 1. Player 2 fakes the drive with the rocker step toward the baseline as 1 begins his jump. Next, 2 rocks back to his initial position and drives past 1 at the exact instant he alights. Player 1 rolls immediately.

Practice this drill from the other side of the floor as well.

Screening with a Post

The other two-man screen involves the post and the point. This is essentially a free-lance drill for a free-lance part of the offense.

In Diagram 12-15 we see 1 dribbling from his point position toward the wing. The difference in this dribble and previous ones is that the dribble is not as shallow but is closer to the post. This dribble signals the post to step out and screen. Player 1 continues past the screen on the drive to the basket, while the post rolls to the basket for the return pass. The post must know whether he is setting a blind screen or not. If he is, then he must allow the player being screened the step to make the screen legal.

This drill should be practiced by all the guards and posts from both sides of the floor until they can execute it properly and easily.

Diagram 12-15

Rebounding Drills

Rebounding for the 1-4 offense should be taught in three phases. One is small group rebounding, another is drill for anticipation, while the third is the application of the first two to the 1-4 offense.

Small Group Rebounding

There is no substitution for small group rebounding drills. Each coach has favorite drills for teaching small group rebounding. These may include three-on-three triangle drills and two-on-one suicide rebounding. They are all good and stress the blockout and move for the ball.

Coaching Anticipation

The Diagrams 12-16 and 12-17 show the 1-4 in two offensive configurations. In each case, you have the ball on the side of the low post, which is the alignment for the power series. You shoot the ball, and the players rush to their assigned rebounding areas as outlined in Chapter 9. Each post rebounds his side of the floor, the ball-side wing rebounds the short middle and the point rebounds the long middle. The off-side wing rotates to the safety position.

The purposes of this drill are to implant the rebounding assignments in the players' heads and to help them learn to anticipate the coming shot.

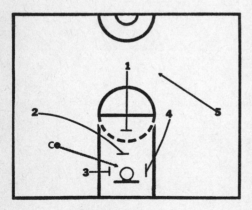

Diagram 12-16   **Diagram 12-17**

Once the players have mastered this drill to the point that they know the assignments and can get to them quickly, defensive players should be added. The drill resumes as a five-on-five rebounding drill with you or the manager shooting. It is helpful to have you or an assistant on the baseline to comment and correct.

Finally, harp at the players during their offensive practice, both in dry-run offensive practice and in live scrimmages, to anticipate when a shot will be taken and to get to their rebounding assignments.

This concludes the section on the 1-4 offense. Drills have not been included in this chapter for the coaching of the shuffle offense since they were detailed in Chapter 4. Nor were drills included for coaching the continuity of free-lance 1-4 offense. The reason it is not included is that free-lance is rule oriented, and if players practice the 1-4 moves they can apply the rules found in Chapter 10 to achieve continuity.

The next section discusses various forms and applications of the presently popular passing game.

PART IV

THE PASSING GAME

13

Coaching
the Passing Game
with a Low Post

"Passing game" and "motion offense" are terms that are used synonymously to identify a group of basketball offenses that are governed by principles rather than by preset patterns. Coaches prefer one name over the other according to the offensive emphasis they wish to communicate to their players. If they wish to emphasize passing without dribbling, then they call it "passing game." However, "motion offense" is usually the term given to the offense when coaches wish to stress the movement of players without the ball.

Because the passing game derives its continuity from principles rather than from predesigned patterns, some coaches call it "freelance offense." However, "free-lance offense" is technically playground basketball and is uncontrolled by either principles or patterns. What coaches really mean is that it is a "freedom offense," because it frees players from the traditional restrictions placed on them by pattern offenses. Players using the passing game are free to choose the passes they make, the receivers they use, the screens they set and the moves they employ to get themselves open. You can add rules to control the shot selection and the dribbling by players who may think that the passing game has liberated them to do their own thing. Coaches need to stress that the passing game is based on the team concept and not on one-on-one basketball. In fact, those coaches who prefer the term "motion offense" wish to emphasize that four players are moving without the basketball rather than just one or two players moving, which so often occurs in traditional pattern basketball.

Advantages and Disadvantages

Because the passing game represents a dramatic departure from traditional offensive basketball, coaches who consider using it should weigh the advantages against the disadvantages.

1. The passing game utilizes four players in addition to the one with the ball, as opposed to one or two players and the one with the ball in traditional pattern offense.

2. The passing game stresses ball movement without dribbling.

3. The passing game provides continuous movement without the necessary recycling that occurs in pattern offense. Time used to recycle an offense is time that the defense can use to regroup.

4. Defensive players learn to anticipate the sequential moves of pattern offenses. The passing game moves are not sequential or preset and are difficult to anticipate.

5. The passing game is difficult to scout. Imagine trying to map an offense that doesn't have set plays.

6. All offensive moves that occur in pattern offense may be incorporated in the passing game.

7. The passing game doesn't require any special type of personnel to make it work.

8. The passing game can be used at all levels of competition.

9. The passing game teaches fundamentals while the offense is being practiced.

10. Offense and defense can be practiced at the same time, because the defense can't "cheat" by anticipating the offensive movement.

11. The passing game can be used with all tempos of play.

12. The passing game can be used effectively against all defenses—man-to-man, zones, match-up zones and combinations.

13. Players like to run the passing game.

While I am unable to discover any disadvantages in the passing game, many coaches are reluctant to use it because they feel that its departure from traditional offense is too radical. They fear loss of floor organization and player control. Ironically, coaches who use the passing game claim the opposite. They are delighted with the discipline that the passing game imposes on their teams. Their players have only five rules to follow, which leads to efficient organization. At any rate, in light of the overwhelming argument in favor of the passing game, you must certainly give it serious consideration in your future planning.

Purposes of the Passing Game

The passing game is an offensive attack, and as such, its purpose is to score. This can be done by either of two methods. The first of these attacks is the deliberate style of play that maneuvers the ball through the waiting defense. The second is the use of the passing game with the fast break as a transition offense. Transition offense is the method of getting into the desired pattern of play following an unsuccessful fast break. Transition offense is discussed in Chapter 14. The passing game can also be used as a delay game, and as such, its purposes are to control possession of the ball, use up time and get the sure basket. However, the passing game emphasizes other purposeful activities.

1. Player movement without the basketball—Since there are no set plays in the passing game, players must create scoring opportunities by moving and by screening without the basketball. The rules governing the passing game (see the next section) encourage all players without the basketball to participate. Conversely, players in pattern offenses are encouraged to wait for predetermined opportunities, which results in reduced player movement.

2. Ball movement without dribbling—Dribbling, as opposed to driving, is rarely purposeful activity. Players use the dribble selfishly, as a means to maintain control of the basketball rather than to create a scoring opportunity. Passing is unselfish and encourages teamwork. Dribbling discourages movement by other players; passing encourages it. Later in this chapter, when the passing game is demonstrated, the reader will notice that screening on the ball is discouraged, because a screen on the ball invites the dribble. This deemphasizes passing, and passing is the name of the game. It should be noted here that driving is purposeful activity when used to take advantage of a defensive error and should be used when the defense dictates. A discussion of when to drive follows in the demonstration of the offense.

3. Team play—It is obvious, from purposes 1 and 2 above, that the passing game fosters team play.

4. Screening for a receiver rather than for a shot—This purpose embodies the main shift in emphasis from traditional basketball. Previously, offenses have been designed to get the jump shooter free. The passing game, however, is intended to find an open player to pass to, which is usually done by screening for him. The offensive thinking behind this purpose is that few, if any, defenses can allow the ball to be reversed on the offensive perimeter two or more times and not break down to the point of yielding the open shot. Traditional offenses look for the shot immediately, seldom having patience to wait for the defensive breakdown. Failing to get the good, quick shot, these offenses often break down themselves.

Rules Governing the Passing Game

Players on the floor need only remember five rules to execute the passing game:

1. Dribble only to penetrate the defense by driving. If you do use your dribble, don't pick up your dribble until you are ready to pass.

2. If the ball is passed (or if the ball is dribbled) to your side as it is brought up the floor, go away and screen to the opposite side of the floor or to the baseline.

3. When you pass the basketball, go to the other side of the floor and screen or go to the baseline and screen.

4. If the screen is set on your defensive man or the player guarding you, then you cut toward the ball.

5. If another cutter is already open in the middle, go back where you came from and screen or get out of the key.

Concerning Formations and Personnel Placement

The low-post passing game operates from the 1-2-2 alignment seen in Diagram 13-1. While exact initial alignment is not necessary to run this offense, a few guidelines are helpful.

Basic Formation

The point guard should be at or near the top of the key. The wings are 1½ steps outside of the free-throw lane, even with the

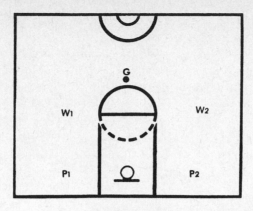

Diagram 13-1

free-throw line extended. This insures them of a good passing lane from the point guard and keeps them from setting up with a foot accidentally in the three-second lane. The posts take positions midway between the foul lane and the sideline and only a step from the baseline. This position allows room for a screen to be set on their man outside the three-second lane, places them in good position to break over the top of a screen, places them in a position where it is difficult for their defensive man to see both them and the ball and keeps the middle open for cutters and drivers.

One of the advantages of the passing game is that it requires no specialty personnel to make it work. Also, no special ball skills are required for the passing game. Since dribbling is discouraged, proficient dribblers are not necessary for offensive success. Clever passing is not required, either. Most of the passes used in the execution of the offense are short, two-handed, overhead lob-passes. Since the passes are being thrown to a receiver rather than to a shooter, they do not have to be thrown into heavy traffic. If you remember that one of the advantages of this offense is that it can be used at any level of competition, you can easily see why this offense is used in many elementary programs and summer camps to teach fundamentals and ball skills.

Personnel Placement

The utilization of players in specific positions does not become a prime consideration in the passing game. Many times, in fact most of the time, the alert coach will, through experimentation, place his players in positions that increase their effectiveness and thereby increase the potency of the offensive attack. Traditionally, the short guard or the best ball handler is placed at the point-guard position. The tall guard (or short forward if a one-guard lineup is to be used) is placed in the W1 slot. The W2 position is usually occupied by the short forward in two-guard lineups or by the tall forward in one-guard lineups. The two taller players occupy the post positions, with the tallest usually in the P2 position. Occasionally, coaches will invert the offense and begin the wings low and the posts high for a vertical screen down on the wings by the posts. This move helps free the wings to begin the offense and puts immediate pressure on the defense when the posts roll inside.

Diagramed Rules for Basic Offensive Movement and Options

It should be mentioned before diagraming the offense that the passing game, because it is a free-lance offense and because it cues itself from defensive pressure, is difficult to illustrate. It should be remembered that, however logical the discussion may be and however sequential the diagrams may be, actual game situations will be much more random and spontaneous. This difference is caused by the defensive pressure applied to the offense. The passing game reacts to defensive pressure, thereby attempting to make the defense readjust and taking advantage of the defense when it is unable to. It is this action, reaction and adjustment which cannot be predicted. Consequently, this diagraming of the passing game will be a rule application of the offensive rules to various defensive situations. The continuity of the offense is derived from the application of these rules and their reapplication as the situation dictates.

Diagram 13-2 illustrates a typical situation that the offense could face as it begins the passing game. The wings and posts have assumed their positions, and the guard, G, has brought the ball into the front court on the dribble and into the good passing area at the top of the key. By keeping the ball in the middle of the floor to begin, the offense has not declared a ball side and a weak side for the defense. Consequently, the defense must play honest defense on their men and cannot sag from the weak side to help the strong side.

The Initial Pass to the Wing

As the ball approaches the area between the center circle and the foul circle in the front court, the wings move to free themselves for

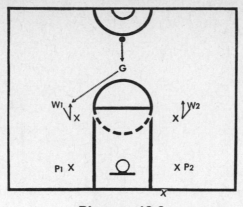

Diagram 13-2

the initial pass. This can be done in a variety of ways, again dictated by the defense. If the defense is playing alongside the wings, they can face their defensive men, walk them back onto their heels and then break to the outside, leaving the defense flatfooted. If the defense is in a denial position on the high side with head and arm in the passing lane, the offensive wings should force the defense to readjust by cutting back-door. When the defense does adjust, the wings should be able to clear easily to the outside. If the defense has overcommitted and cannot adjust, then, of course, the guard should pass the ball to the open wing for the obvious scoring opportunity. Finally, if the defense is playing the wings on the low side or slightly behind them, the wings should lock the defense on their backs by simply stepping in front of them, giving a target for the pass and moving quickly to meet the ball when it is thrown.

Diagram 13-2 shows the wings freeing themselves. Player G, who has not picked up his dribble yet, as this is an important principle, moves away from his defensive man, who is overplaying him slightly to the left, to pass the ball to W1. Normally, this pass to either wing initiates the offense.

The Option to Drive

However, before this play is pursued any further, the possibility of G beating his man with the quick drive needs to be explored. Diagram 13-3 shows that the wings have made their preliminary moves and that G has beaten his defensive man by using the drive. The wings, seeing that G is driving, flare to the outside to clear the middle of the key and give him room. Player G, using sound basket-

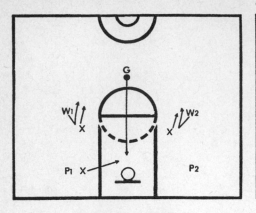 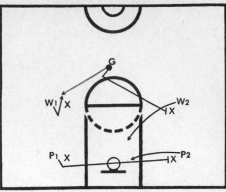

Diagram 13-3   **Diagram 13-4**

ball judgment, continues his drive until he is picked up or until he scores. Diagram 13-3 shows the defensive man leaving P1 to stop G. Player G feeds off to P1 who should score easily on the lay-up.

The Horizontal Screen Away from the Ball

Returning to the original play, Diagram 13-4 shows G completing his pass to W1. Player G now applies Principle 3. Having passed to one side of the floor, he goes to the other side and screens for W2. Likewise, P1 applies Principle 2 as he goes away from the ball and screens. P2 and W2 are shown breaking over the top of the screens set for them. One of them must now apply Principle 5. Since another cutter is in the middle, stay out of the key. Experienced coaches will notice that W2 will probably have to apply the principle. P1 left to set his screen immediately upon completion of the pass to W1. Player G, on the other hand, took two steps toward the ball to create a give-and-go threat (which should be used if the defense doesn't readjust) and to improve his screening angle against W2's man. Consequently G's screen will be later in arriving than P1's. If P2 is open, he should get the ball for the attempt at the basket. If not, W2, noting that P2 is already in the middle, elects to get out of the key (Principle 5) and gets the ball from W1. (Diagram 13-5) W1 and P2 now apply Principles 3 and 2 respectively and go away to screen. P2 must clear the key to get a new three-second count before recrossing the lane to screen.

Diagram 13-6 depicts a variation of the same play, seen in Diagram 13-4. The chief difference is that the men covering on W2 and P2 are shown playing on the high side of their men in order that they might be in position to fight over the top of the screens. W2 and P2

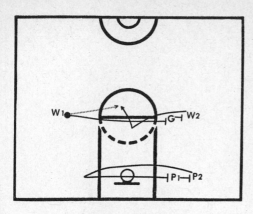

Diagram 13-5

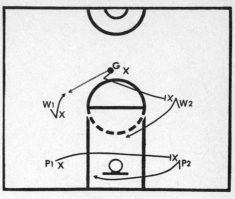

Diagram 13-6

see this, start over the top and then back-cut behind the screens. This practice of going away from the defensive pressure is very important to the success of the passing game. It is very important that the screener and the player for whom he is screening work together against the defense. Some guidelines for screening procedure are in order at this point.

How to Screen for the Passing Game

Generally, the two-footed jump-stop screen is preferred. The screener, who is running toward his defensive target must leave the floor with a one-footed jump and land with a two-footed jump-stop in a legal screening position. Legal screening position means that he must be facing the player to be screened and be far enough from him so that the player being screened is able to stop. This screening procedure will take practice, and you must be prepared to endure a few early season practices filled with illegal screens.

The player for whom the screen is being set must learn to time his move as well. He must be aware of the position that the defense has assumed against him. If the defense is playing him to the high side, he will want to go low on a back-cut. If the defense is playing him low, he will want to go over the top. As the screener leaves the floor, at the precise instant that the one-footed jump has begun but while the foot is still on the floor, the player getting the screen jab-steps in the direction of the defense, crosses over as the screener lands and goes opposite, This execution will leave the defensive man cleanly and legally screened.

Switching by the defense is inevitable. Consequently, the

screener must roll at the precise instant that the offensive cutter (the man from whom the screen was set) leaves the screener's peripheral vision. There is one exception to this, however. When switches occur at the wing, the screener rolls immediately upon landing; jump, stop and roll are effected in rapid succession. This move will open up many scoring opportunities for the screener in the middle of the key.

Technique for Screening in the Key

One other screening technique deserves mention here. Screening from the 1-2-2 formation means that screens must sometimes be set in the key. The three-second rule is a factor that makes the roll difficult. Diagram 13-7 illustrates the move at the post position. P1 must execute a screen against the man guarding P2. This defensive man is shown sagging off P2 and in the lane. P1 moves across the lane, times his jump and lands in good screening position, although at a slightly oblique angle to the defensive man. In fact, P1 is facing the corner where the boundary of the foul lane meets the baseline. P2 cuts past P1 and P1 lands. P1 then picks up his right foot (designated R in the diagram), pivots upon his left (designated L in the diagram), crosses over and steps out of the lane with his right foot. He then lifts his left foot, but does not remove it from the lane, pushes off with his right foot and steps back down in the lane with his left foot. He has now broken the three-second count and initiated his roll. This technique works equally well at the wing position.

Again, switching is inevitable, therefore rolling must be insisted upon. It is a wise rule that says, "Roll a minimum of two steps, more if

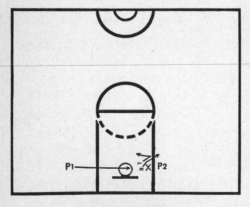

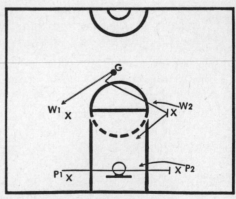

Diagram 13-7   **Diagram 13-8**

you are open. If you are not open, assume the position vacated by your teammate who used your screen." The roll is demonstrated in Diagram 13-8.

The Continuity of the Low-Post Passing Game

The basic low-post passing game has now been demonstrated: pass, go away to screen-and-roll. If no scoring opportunity presents itself, repeat the process: pass, go away to screen-and-roll. Of course, the threats of the give-and-go and of the drive are always present. As is apparent, the passing game is an amazingly simple continuity offense to learn and run. For the defense, however, it is infinitely various and complex. The defense must guard against the cut, the drive, fight over screens, switch and contend with mismatches. It must adjust, readjust and adjust again. Eventually, the assignments become confused, players get lost in traffic, mismatches occur or reactions are impaired. The defense becomes vulnerable. Remember that modern offensive thinking maintains that the defense must be moved before it can be penetrated. The passing game does this.

Occasionally, the defense is able to cover the offense for a complete series while the offense passes and goes away to screen-and-roll. If no receivers are open and the ball is not passed, the rollers balance the floor by assuming the positions of their teammates for whom they screened. The players cutting off screens to the ball reverse and go away from the ball to screen again. It is imperative that, for just such a situation, the player with the ball save his dribble. He can now use it to drive if he is being swamped by his defensive man, or he may use it to get a new 5-second count. Once he uses his dribble, however, he should not pick the ball up until he is ready to pass. This action is seen in Diagram 13-9.

Combating Half-Court Pressure

Some defenses, not wishing to try to keep up with the passing game once it gets underway, put intense pressure on the offense at all points trying to cause a turnover on the first pass. When this happens, several counters are available to the offense.

First, spread the offense. This opens the middle up for the offense to operate and negates the possibility of defensive help there. Since the defense is overplaying, it is vulnerable to the drive, the back-door cut and the give-and-go. The open middle insures the

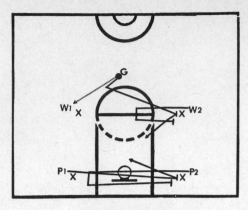

Diagram 13-9

success of these moves. A maximum spread would be one that deployed the wings and posts midway between the foul lane and the sidelines.

Second, encourage one-on-one play by the point guard and by the wings. Since these players are facing intense pressure when they have the ball, often to the point of defensive overplay, the quick drive stands a good chance of success. The wings may be more successful at this than the point guard. The point usually draws the quicker better defensive player, for one thing. Also, his defensive man will usually try to guard against the drive by playing directly in front of him. The wings, on the other hand, have a natural driving angle to the basket, and they are usually overplayed from one side, making it easier to drive. When the wings do drive, they are, by virtue of their position, one position closer to the basket than the point. Because of this, the only defensive man who can help is the defensive post on that side. When the point guard drives, he faces possible coverage from the defensive wings and posts on both sides. Regardless of who makes the move the result is the same; the defense has been penetrated.

Third, change the point of entry into the offense. This is shown in Diagram 13-10. The point guard dribbles the ball to the wing position to initiate the offense instead of passing the ball there. This neutralizes the pressure on the first pass. Applying Principle 2, P1 and W1 go away and screen, and the offense is underway in spite of intense pressure.

Finally, change the point at which the screens are set to initiate the offense as shown in Diagram 13-11. To counter the overplay at the wings, have the wings screen down vertically on the posts. The posts now break to the wing positions for the pass that initiates the offense.

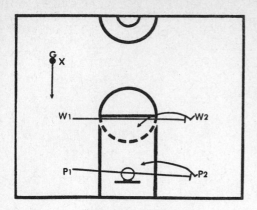 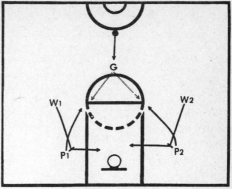

Diagram 13-10   **Diagram 13-11**

The vertical screen is an extremely difficult move to defend. The result is that the posts are open to pass to. Note that the wings roll inside to put immediate pressure on the defense. Many coaches begin the passing game with the posts at the wing positions and then screen down to begin the offense. This ploy provides good transition from the defensive end of the floor, as the taller players usually stay for rebounds and have the furthest distance to travel coming back for offense. Upon arriving, they can go immediately into the vertical screen and start the offense. An added benefit is that the defense may be forced to switch. Since the shorter wings are at the post positions, the switch gives the offense the immediate advantage of having shorter players defending the taller posts near the basket. It should be noted here that "Go away and screen . . ." in Principle 2 includes the vertical screen in Diagram 13-11 as well as the horizontal screen in Diagram 13-4. By simply including the vertical screen in the offense, you make the offense much more varied and difficult to defend.

Combating Sagging Defenses

Against sagging defenses or sloughing defenses, the offense should shrink next to the key to take up the slack. This constriction increases traffic in the middle. Traffic causes the defense to get hung up, even though the defense may have been sloughing to avoid screens.

Occasionally, these sloughing defenses switch too soon while trying to avoid the screen-and-roll. Diagram 13-12 illustrates a move that is effective when the defensive wings refuse to defend their men on the vertical screen. They have stopped in anticipation of the cut to

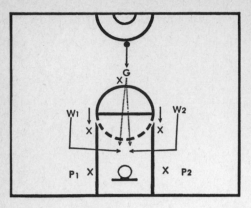 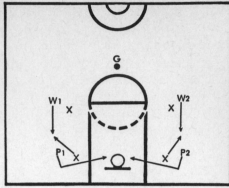

Diagram 13-12   **Diagram 13-13**

the ball by P1 and P2. Seeing this, W1 and W2 do not set the screens
but cut to the middle. This move places them behind their men and
leaves them undefended. Diagram 13-13 depicts a similar action at
the post positions. The defensive posts, in anticipation of the coming
switch on the vertical screen, leave early to pick up their new man on
the exchange. P1 and P2 see this and cut behind them to the basket.

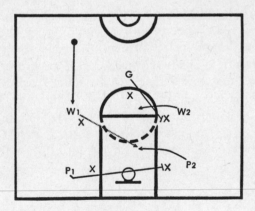

Diagram 13-14

Of course, there is a point when sagging or sloughing man-to-
man defenses become zones. When this happens, you may wish to
run the keep-away game described in Chapter 16. If not, continue
with the passing game, but enter the ball on the dribble into a gap
between two defenders. Make the two defenders take the man with

the ball while the offensive players on the ball side go away and screen, as previously demonstrated. Since the defensive players on the opposite side of the floor may not be in man-for-man coverage, the screeners may have to screen the man in a general area or zone. Also, it is helpful against zones to enter the ball at a wing and then look to reverse it quickly as shown in Diagram 13-14. At any rate, the defense is no longer pressure defense, which the passing game was meant to destroy.

14

Coaching
the Passing Game
with a High Post

Like the low-post passing game described in Chapter 13, the high-post passing game is a rule offense, that is, the players' movements on the floor are governed by rules rather than by set offensive plays. Because of its offensive freedom, the high-post passing game stresses passing, player movement away from the ball and off-ball screening. It discourages dribbling for the sake of dribbling. In fact, it has all of the advantages given the low-post passing game in Chapter 13, plus a few more.

Advantages of the High-Post Passing Game

1. Because of its 1-3-1 alignment the high-post passing game leaves much of the floor cleared out for driving, particularly by the wings.

2. Because of its high-low post alignment it encourages post play to get the good inside shot. It is a particularly good offense to use if the high post can drive or if you have a very tall player and want to keep him next to the basket.

3. The high-post passing game is more effective against match-up zones than the low-post passing game.

4. Because its initial alignment is similar to the player configuration at the end of a fast break, it makes a good transitional offense. A

transitional offense is one that moves a team easily from the unsuccessful fast break into their normal pattern or style of play. Some coaches call this the secondary break because the shots that come from this transitional phase are not a part of the fast break, but they are not a part of the normal offense either.

5. The high-post passing game provides good open avenues for offensive rebounding.

6. Because its initial alignment is similar to the player configuration at the end of a fast break, it blends well with the fast break.

7. When used in conjunction with the low-post passing game, the 1-4, or similar offense, it provides a "different look" for the offense. This is a very real disadvantage for the defense. They have to defend what they feel is totally new offense, while the offense merely changed alignments. The offensive rules for the high-post passing game are nearly the same as those for the low-post passing game.

Disadvantages of the High-Post Passing Game

1. Players and their positions are not usually as interchangeable in the high-post passing game as they are in the low-post passing game. Post players are usually designated as such, taught as such and substituted as such, thereby separating the team into posts and non-posts. This creates a further disadvantage when the posts assume their positions on the floor time after time. Their defensive men grow accustomed to looking for them in the same areas and can relax a bit on defense.

2. The high-post passing game is slightly more restricted in its movement than the low-post passing game.

Rules for the High-Post Passing Game

One of the differences of the high-post passing game is that it has separate sets of rules for the post players and for the outside players. The wings and the point guard have one set of rules, while the posts operate from another set. This is not a problem, however, since both sets of rules are similar and since there are only five rules in each set. Here are the rules for the outside players:

Rules for the Non-Post Players

1. Dribble only to penetrate by driving to the basket; if a defensive player picks you up on your drive to the basket, dump the ball off to the open man.

2. If you pass and cut to the basket and do not receive the ball, you must assume a position on the opposite side of the floor from where you passed the ball.

3. If you pass and do not cut to the basket, go away from your pass and screen.

4. If a screen is set on your defensive man or on the defensive player guarding you, cut to the ball.

5. Back-cut, that is break to the basket behind your defensive man, on all overplays. Wings should translate this into never coming higher than the free-throw line extended to get the ball from the point guard. If you are a wing and can't get the pass from the point without breaking above the free-throw line extended, then back-cut.

Rules for the Post Players

1. If the ball is passed to your side of the floor, go to the other side of the floor and screen.

2. If a cutter cuts past you or through your area, post-up and keep a passing lane open to the ball.

3. If the ball is passed to the other post, break to the basket.

4. If a screen is set on your defensive man or on the defensive player guarding you, break to the ball.

5. Back-cut on all overplays by your defensive man.

Following a brief discussion of player and position requirements, all of these rules will be applied and thoroughly illustrated.

Concerning Formations and Personnel Placement

The high-post passing game operates from a 1-3-1 formation, as mentioned earlier. This formation is shown in Diagram 14-1.

Basic Formation

The point guard is at or near the top of the key. It is important that he not pick up his dribble too far out, since his teammates at the wings are a good distance from him and since long passes are more easily intercepted by the defense.

The wings take a position that is equidistant between the foul lane and the sideline and between the baseline and the free-throw

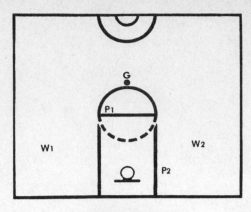

Diagram 14-1

line extended. Sometimes it is helpful for the wings to be nearer the baseline since that position is more difficult to defend. The position of the wings as illustrated in Diagram 14-1 gives them optimum passing lanes from the point guard and to both post men. These passing lanes are important because the ball must be moved by passing quickly to the open man.

The posts assume positions on either side of the key, but opposite from each other. Usually it is advantagious for the low post to set up on the left side of the key, as shown in Diagram 14-1, so that he can break to his right for the basket. The low post should be next to the lower, block-shaped hash mark on the side of the foul lane. The high post is above the free-throw line. Usually, he keeps at least one foot in the upper half of the foul circle.

Personnel Placement

Generally, the tallest player will occupy the low post position to provide rebounding strength and to take advantage of his height next to the basket. If not, the tallest, least mobile player should be utilized here. The high post should be played by one of the taller players on the floor. He should be able to drive a bit and it is a real bonus for your offensive thrust if he can score with the jump shot from the free-throw line.

The three outside positions are played by the smaller, quicker players. They should be the best ball handlers on the team. The best ball handler of the three usually plays the point guard since he brings the ball up the floor and initiates the offense.

Diagramed Rules for
Basic Offensive Movement and Options

To repeat a major point made in Chapter 13, however logical the discussion (of the passing game) may be, actual game situations will be much more random and spontaneous. With this in mind, here are the diagramed movements of the high-post passing game. The rules for the outside players are discussed separately from those for the posts.

Beginning with the outside players and reviewing the initial alignment in Diagram 14-1, notice that the point guard is at or near the top of the key. Advancement to this position is crucial to the successful operation of the high-post passing game. This is the reason for placing a good ball handler in this position so that the ball can be advanced should there be stiff defensive pressure. Noting that the three elements that determine whether a pass will be successful or not are distance, angle and velocity, it is apparent that because of the deep positioning of the wings the ball must be advanced to the top of the key to shorten the distance the ball must travel should it be passed to either of the wings.

While the wings are a good distance from the point guard, their positioning midway between the foul lane and the sideline, is wide enough to provide a good, open passing angle from the point guard. They should be at least as deep as the midpoint between the baseline and the foul-line extended. This position places them approximately midway between the posts so that if they get the ball they have good passing angles to either post. It may be necessary for the wings to set lower, initially, then shown in Diagram 14-1 so that they can move to get open. For instance, in Diagram 14-2, the wings are set lower,

Diagram 14-2

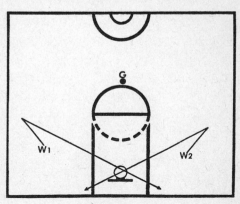

Diagram 14-3

break toward the baseline to turn their men around and then break
clear to receive the pass from the point. If the defense overplays them
as they break to the outside, then they apply Rule 5 and back-cut as
shown in Diagram 14-3. If the defensive men guarding the wings play
behind their men, the wings can simply break over the top of them to
receive the pass from the point in good scoring area as shown in
Diagram 14-4. This concludes the discussion of bringing the ball into
the high-post passing game at the point and moving the wings to open
them for a pass to initiate the offense. Now to the actual application of
the rules.

Initiation of the Offense with the Drive

Rule 1 states, "Dribble only to penetrate by driving to the basket. If a defensive player picks you up on your drive to the basket,
dump the ball off to the open man." Diagram 14-5 shows driving
penetration by the point guard who is able to get past his man.
Applying this rule he passes to the open man, in this case to the high
post when another defender moves to pick him up. Had no one
picked him up, the guard would have continued to the basket.

Diagram 14-6 illustrates the same application of the rule from the
wing. The point guard passes to W2 at the wing when he breaks clear.
W2 then drives on his man and passes to P2, the low post, who is
open because his man moves to stop W2. In situations other than this
kind of penetration, no dribbling should be permitted. A good coaching point is to remind outside players to look for the drive but not to
attempt it if there is no clear opportunity to do so. Remind them that
this is the passing game, and passing will set up other opportunities.

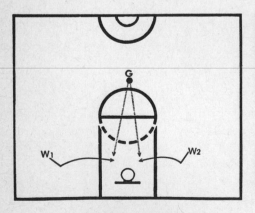

Diagram 14-4

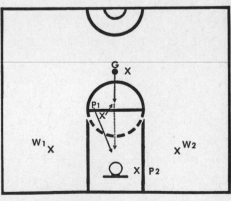

Diagram 14-5

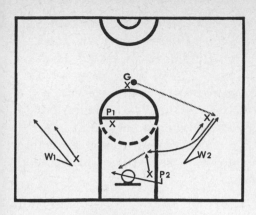
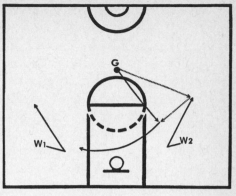

Diagram 14-6   **Diagram 14-7**

Initiation of the Offense with the Pass

If no drive presents itself to the point guard, then he can pass and cut to the basket as stated in Rule 2. Diagram 14-7 shows this application with a simple give-and-go by the point guard. Notice that the offside wing, W1, moves to the point for balance and for the option of a return pass by W2. If W2 is unable to get the ball to G on the give-and-go, then G must apply the rest of Rule 2. He continues through the key and then turns away from the ball to take a position opposite his pass. This position is open because the wing, W1, has moved to the point.

Diagram 14-8 shows a variation of the same rule application. G passes to W1 this time and begins to go away. (Note: G seems to be applying Rule 3 as he starts toward the other side of the floor after he passes to W1.) G abruptly cuts back toward the ball for the pass. This

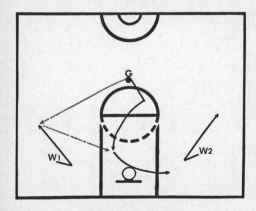
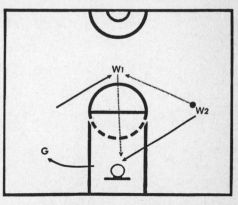

Diagram 14-8   **Diagram 14-9**

move is called the jab-and-go to differentiate it from the give-and-go. It is especially effective after Rule 3 has been applied a few times.

Diagram 14-9 shows Rule 2 applied from the wing. W2 has the ball, G has cut to the basket as shown in Diagram 14-7 and W1 has moved to the top of the key. W2 executes a give-and-go with W1. Perhaps the option most used by the outside men is the one resulting from Rule 3 which states, "If you pass and do not cut to the basket, then go away from your pass and screen." G does this in Diagram 14-10. He passes to W1 who has cleared himself to the outside, and then G goes opposite to screen for W2.

How to Screen for the High-Post Passing Game

In the high-post passing game as in the low-post passing game, the screening technique is important. It is important that all moves be executed at full or close to full speed. In Diagram 14-10, G breaks toward W2 at full speed and then sets his screen by executing a two-footed jump-stop. This is done by leaving the floor with one foot from a running jump and landing on both feet in good screening position. This technique must be practiced and coordinated with W2 who now employs Rule 4.

Seeing a screener coming toward his man, W2 makes a jab at the baseline to set up his defensive man. At the precise instant that G leaves the floor with one foot to begin his jump-screen, W2 breaks over the top of the screen for the resulting lay-up as shown in Diagram 14-10.

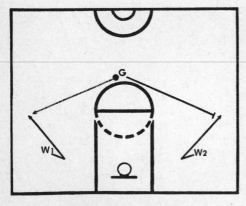

Diagram 14-10

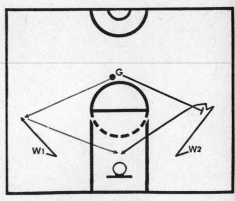

Diagram 14-11

Combating the Switch in the High-Post Passing Game

Switching by the defense against the high-post passing game is inevitable. Diagram 14-11, which is an option of the pass-and-go-away-and-screen rule, is the most obvious counter to switching dy the defense. G passes to W1 and goes opposite to screen for W2. W2 cuts over the top of the screen, receives the pass from W1 and takes the jump shot before G's defensive man is able to switch and cover him.

Defensive switching at the wings can be countered in this manner several times, but the temptation by G's defensive man to leave early, so as to stop the jump shot, must be anticipated. Outside players should be alerted to the option available in Diagram 14-12. The availability of this option is always present against a defense that constantly switches to stop the outside jump shot. However, players must be coached and drilled in practice to read and react to the early switch by G's defensive man.

In Diagram 14-12, G goes opposite to screen, but his man either leaves early or trails G into the screen in anticipation of W2 coming over the top of the screen. Seeing no defensive man to his inside, G, immediately upon landing with both feet in good screening position, reverse-pivots on his baseline foot and rolls down the key for the scoring pass from W1.

Finally, the outside players in the high-post passing game must be prepared to react to the eventuality of W2's defensive man fighting over the top of the screen set by G. To do so, the defensive player at the wing must cheat a half step or so to the high side of W2 as G is coming to set the screen. At the precise instant that G is landing in his jump-screening position, W2 back-cuts to the basket as shown in Diagram 14-13.

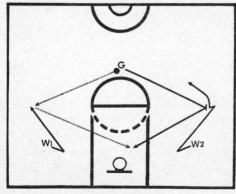

Diagram 14-12

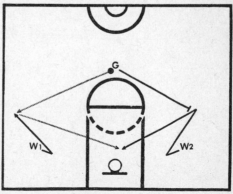

Diagram 14-13

Coaching Hints for Outside Players

These, then, are the options most often available to the outside players in the high-post passing game. At this point, continuity, floor balance and patience need to be stressed. Many times, the first pass, and sometimes the second, will not result in a scoring opportunity. In fact, against good defensive teams the ball will have to be passed along the outside perimeter four or more times before the scoring opportunity develops. A good coaching point here to insure movement, balance and continuity is that a player should occupy a stationary position for only one second before reapplying one of the rules and moving to a new position.

One final coaching hint needs mentioning before discussing post play. If a wing passes to the point and there is no one that he can screen on his side of the floor, or if no one sets a screen for him, then he must do one of two things. He must either cut to the basket and, failing to receive the ball, continue to the baseline at full speed and return to his original position or, after cutting to the basket, he must continue across he key and screen for someone there.

Coaching Post Play in the High-Post Passing Game

It is helpful to introduce the high-post passing game to the outside players separately from the post players. During early season practices, much introduction and coaching of the offense through drills can be done with the outside players at one end of the floor while the posts are learning their portion of the high-post passing game at the other end.

When teaching the posts the offense, it is important that they apply the rules and learn the offense from both the high and the low-post positions even though you might wish that one of them spend most of his time at the low-post position. You will find that they must interchange at some point in the operation of the offense. With this in mind, here are the rules applications for the posts.

Rule 1 for the posts says, "If the ball is passed to your side of the floor, then go away and screen." Diagram 14-14 shows the ball being passed to W1 who is on the same side of the floor as the high post, P1. P1 now has the option to go away and screen for the opposite wing or for the low post, P2, as in Diagram 14-15. If P1 screens for P2, then P2 must apply Rule 4, "If a screen is set on your defensive man or on the defensive player guarding you, break to the ball." Remember that

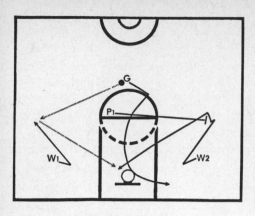 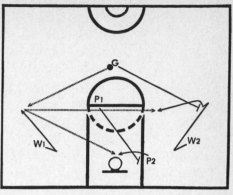

Diagram 14-14   **Diagram 14-15**

the outside men are applying their rules simultaneously with the posts. For instance, G executed a jab-and-go in Diagram 14-14 after passing to the wing. In Diagram 14-15, he went away and screened for P2 at the wing.

   Diagram 14-16 illustrates the ball being passed to the same side of the floor that the low post, P2, is on. P2 applies Rule 1 and goes away to screen for the other post. P1 now applies Rule 4 and breaks off the screen to the ball.

   In Diagram 14-17, P2 goes away to screen for W1. Notice that in this instance G happened to choose to screen for W1 as well, which is perfectly all right. It simply shows that, in the high-post passing game, there will be instances where double screens occur. In fact, double screens happen regularly in this offense.

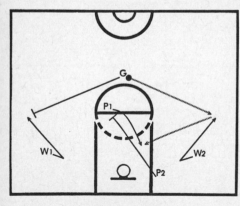 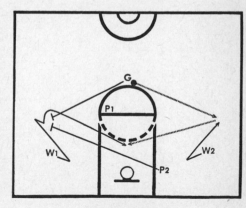

Diagram 14-16   **Diagram 14-17**

One coaching hint here is that the posts may have to interchange to keep the floor balance. In Diagram 14-16, P2 would be the high post after his screen while P1 would be the low post after cutting off the screen to the basket. In Diagram 14-17 the posts do not interchange, but P1 should assume a position at the other side of the key after hesitating for one second. He does this by applying Rule 2, "If a cutter cuts past you or through your area, post up and keep a passing lane open to the ball." When P1 breaks to the other side of the key, toward W2 who has the ball, he may be open for a pass from W2. If he receives the ball as in Diagram 14-18, then Rule 3 is applied by P2. Rule 3 says, "If the ball is passed to the other post, break to the basket." A good, quick move may open P2 in the lane for the post-to-post pass and a resulting one-on-one move to the basket. W2 must remember to apply one of his rules immediately upon passing the ball.

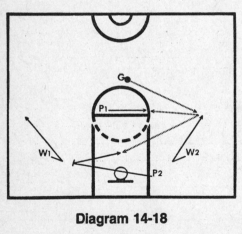

Diagram 14-18

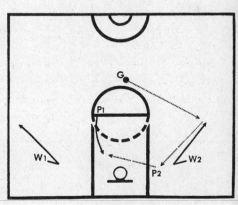

Diagram 14-19

A similar application of Rule 3 could have occurred before P2 went to the other side of the floor to screen. Remember that any play has a full second to allow something to develop before applying the rules. Diagram 14-19 shows the ball being passed to W2 at the wing. W2 passes to P2 at the low post and P1 breaks to the basket while W2 applies one of his rules.

Two other possible illustrations of Rule 2 are shown in Diagram 14-20. G passes to W2 before executing a jab-and-go. Since G cut through P1's area, P1 posts up on the ball side. If he receives a pass as shown, then P2 applies Rule 3 and cuts to the basket. G, who did not receive a pass comes out of the key away from the ball. W1 moves to the point for balance. W2 must remember to apply a rule, following his pass to the post.

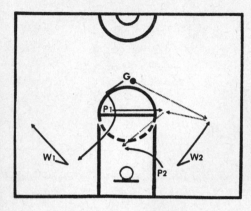
Diagram 14-20

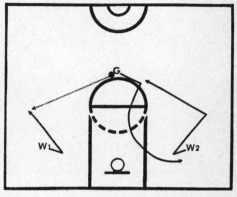
Diagram 14-21

In Diagram 14-21 G passes to W1. His subsequent jab-and-go moves him through both P1 and P2's areas. Both P1 and P2 post where they stand, having applied Rule 2. As the ball is reversed, as shown in Diagram 14-22, it may be passed to P1 from W2 at the point or to P2 from G at the wing.

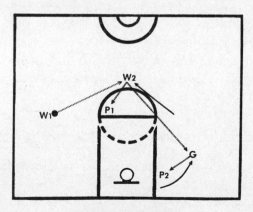
Diagram 14-22

Finally, Rule 5 is self-explanatory. However, one application is illustrated to show the reaction of both posts. In Diagram 14-23, P1's defensive man is playing very high to discourage a pass from the point to the high post. P1 applies Rule 5 and cuts to the basket. This can happen as the ball is passed to W1 as shown in Diagram 14-23 or before W1 gets the pass. The rule must be applied in either situation. The difference is that P1 will score if W1 has the ball and can get it to him. If W1 doesn't have the ball, then P1 takes the low-post position. Notice that P2 breaks to the high-post position. He will be open for the pass from the point if G has not already passed the ball. If G has passed to W1, P2 remains at high post and the offense continues from there.

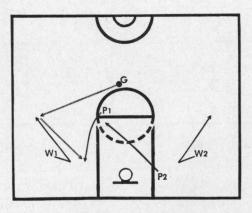

Diagram 14-23

One final coaching hint, before leaving this discussion of basic offensive movement, comes in the form of a reminder that many basketball games are won by getting the ball to the posts. The high-post passing game provides excellent opportunities to get the ball inside. As the ball is passed along the perimeter, the outside men must be conscious of the movement of the posts inside. A bit of patience and good passing will result in the high percentage shots near the basket.

Rebounding the High-Post Passing Game

Here are the rules that provide good rebounding positions in the high-post passing game.

1. Each post rebounds his side of the basket.

2. Whoever occupies the wing positions rebounds in the middle of the key.

3. Whoever is at the point when a shot is taken stays back for defense.

High-Post Passing Game as a Transitional Offense

As mentioned previously, one of the advantages of the high-post passing game is that it provides excellent transition from the fast break to the normal style of play. Most coaches divide the game of basketball into two elements—offense and defense. This delineation, however, neglects the portion of the game wherein the players switch ends of the floor. In this portion of the game the offense is not yet established, nor is the defense set. Both are in transition, either from defense to offense or from offense to defense, hence the term transitional. Since much time is spent in transition, that portion of the game deserves attention. Preparation for organized transition can provide a distinct advantage for a team. The high-post passing game provides smooth transition, especially for the fast breaking team. Furthermore, to take full advantage of the transitional phase of the game, a team must fast break.

The Transition Game Illustrated

Diagram 14-24 illustrates the transitional game using the high-post passing game. Rebounding from a 2-1-2 set for purposes of illustration F1, the forward on defense passes to G1 to begin the fast break. G1 passes to G2, who brings the ball into the front court. G1 fills the left lane of the pattern break, while F2 fills the right lane. P is the trailer, and F1, who rebounded, is the safety. If the fast break is unsuccessful, the offensive players quickly prepare for the transitional phase of their offense. Notice where the players deploy themselves in Diagram 14-24. The player who brought the ball to the point, in this case G2, becomes the point guard. G1 and F2, the players who filled the outside lanes during the fast break become the wings. The first post down the floor, the trailer, who in this case was unable to help produce the fast break basket, becomes the low post. The last post to arrive is the high post. The wings, who failed to get the basket from the outside lanes, break to the outside to initiate the high-post passing game, as illustrated, and the offense is underway. The only coaching hints needed here are that the player at the point must not hold the ball but must find an open teammate as soon as possible and then apply one of the rules. It may happen that he can pass to one of the players in the outside fast-break lanes before they break out, or he can even pass to the trailer before he gets to his low-post position. If neither can score, execution of the rules from that point will provide smooth, quick transition to offense. The experienced coach will immediately notice a real advantage to this quick transition. The defense is not yet set, and resulting defensive confusion should help produce the easy basket that the fast break could not.

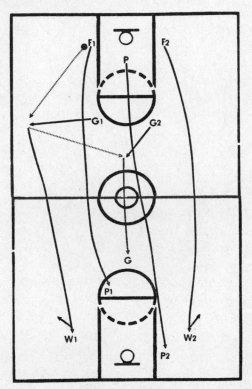

Diagram 14-24

Finally, all of this rule application may seem a bit frightening to you if you haven't tried the passing game, but the dividends are not long in coming. Just remember to teach the rules through drills (drills for coaching the passing game are given in Chapter 15) and be patient until the players become accustomed to reacting to the rules and to each other's movements. Don't let them stand around and beg for the ball. Enforce the "one second and move" rule. They'll soon enjoy the offense, and that makes your job easier.

15

Incorporating
the Passing Game
Through Drills

Of the four offenses contained in this book, the passing game is the most difficult to teach through drills. Since the passing game has no set pattern, drills are used to teach fundamentals rather than plays themselves, The reason for the shift of emphasis from plays to fundamentals is that the passing game has no set plays to teach because it relies on the application of rules and the use of fundamental skills. The drills used, then, are those that teach skills that are most used in the passing game. All of the drills utilize the offensive configuration of the passing game to insure carry-over to the operation of the offense.

Shooting Drills

Players shoot enough on their own so that their shooting is fairly well practiced. It is very important for the scheduled practice time alloted to shooting to be specifically devoted to the particular moves and shots most commonly used in the passing game. It is important that all of the players practice all of the moves and shoot all of the shots so that they get some experience from various positions within the offense. The only exception to this premise might occur when using the high-post passing game. Here, you may wish to have the posts learn their inside shots and moves before freeing some of their practice time to practice from the outside. However, it is important for all of the players to practice the post position because it teaches them how to get good position inside and how to cut back against overplays. It also makes them conscious of what constitutes good post position and of the timing needed between post and outside player for the ball to be passed inside.

Generally, I don't teach offense for the first week. Nor do I use drills that are team oriented towards offense for the first week. I do, however, use some of the shooting drills from the first day on. I begin practice each day with two lay-up drills and two jump shot drills. Since I use these drills all season long, I try not to let them last too long each day—perhaps 2 1/2 minutes per each shooting drill. Aside from emphasizing good shooting and passing techniques, emphasis should be placed on executing the drills at full speed. Players should not become reckless and should remain under control. I also emphasize sharp turns and straight-line cuts rather than rounded "rainbow" arcs.

Teaching the Give-and-Go

Diagram 15-1 illustrates a give-and-go lay-up drill. The squad is divided into three lines. A passes to B and then executes the give-and-go move in a straight-line cut to the basket. C rebounds and passes the ball back to line A at the point. C follows his pass to take a place at the end of line A. A goes to line B after his lay-up. B goes to the rebound line.

In order to simulate situations encountered in games, we vary this drill slightly from day to day. At the beginning of the season, we have A initiate the drill by advancing the ball on the dribble at half speed. As in the illustration in Diagram 15-1, A passes to B off his left foot (his inside foot) and accelerates to full speed, using the momentum gained when he pushed off to pass the ball. This move utilizes A's forward momentum to propel him past the imaginary defensive player. Emphasize the straight-line cut, as it is the shortest distance to the basket.

The other game situation that needs simulating is to have A execute the give-and-go from a stationary position, A passes to B and then decoys his imaginary defensive player so that the defense will relax. This is done by having A straighten up after his pass and then walk two seps, beginning with his inside foot again. When the inside foot comes down for the second time, A pushes off with it and accelerates toward the basket. The theory here is that even if the defense doesn't relax, A's two steps will place him so close to the defensive player that the defensive player can't react in time to regain defensive position.

This drill should be run to both sides. For variety, later in the year, A can shoot the jump shot after receiving the return pass from B.

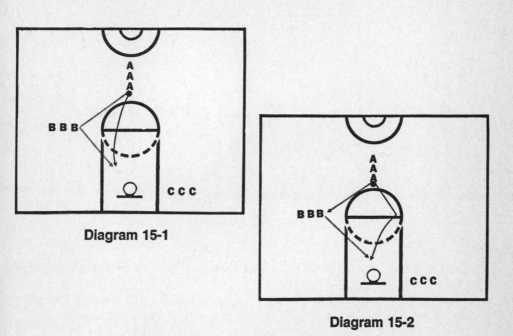

Diagram 15-1

Diagram 15-2

Teaching the Jab-and-Go

The drill for teaching the jab-and-go move is seen in Diagram 15-2. This drill is set up exactly like the one for teaching the give-and-go in Diagram 15-1. A's move, however, is again the main point of emphasis. A can initiate this drill either fron the dribble or from the standing position. He goes away from his pass at least four steps before cutting back for the return pass. A's move away is done at full speed, as is his back-cut. A's back-cut is initiated either by the quick sharp turn or by the reverse-pivot method. I emphasize these moves and have my players practice them on alternating days. This drill should be run to both sides and can be varied with the jump shot instead of the lay-up.

Drilling Back-Door Situations

Diagram 15-3 shows the back-door drill or back-cut drill. Here A is passing to B for the lay-up, but not until B has touched the corner of the foul lane and then started his back-cut to the basket. C is the rebounder again, with the players rotating in counterclockwise fashion.

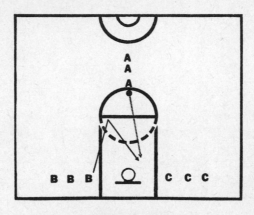

Diagram 15-3

This drill simulates a game situation wherein B is overplayed as he breaks to the ball. Applying a passing game rule, he back-cuts to the basket on the overplay and never comes higher than the free-throw line to receive a pass from the point. B's entire move is done at full speed. His back-cut should be via one of three moves. Only one of these moves should be practiced by the team at a time.

The first of these moves is the sharp cut off the outside foot and accleration to the opposite side of the basket. The second of these moves by B is the reverse pivot off the inside foot to lock the defensive player behind him and push off the same inside foot toward the opposite side of the basket. Thirdly, when B arrives at the foul line, he is at the high-post position. To simulate post play in this drill, especially for our post players, we have them execute a two-footed jump-stop at the foul line, catch the ball, reverse-pivot on the inside foot and drive to the basket.

This drill is one of my favorites. I run it to both sides. Beginning with the second week of the season, I add a fourth line to play defense on B. The timing of the pass from A to B then becomes critically important, as does the pass itself. It is also a very good drill for pressure defense. It hones the defensive reflexes and teaches the defense not to be afraid to gamble with the back-cut early in the season.

Diagram 15-4 is a simple drill, but it is very effective. It is a natural extension of the back-cut drill in Diagram 15-3. A completes the pass to B, this time before he gets to the foul-line extended so that

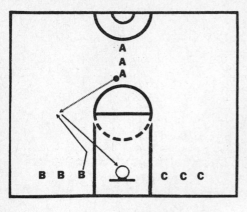

Diagram 15-4

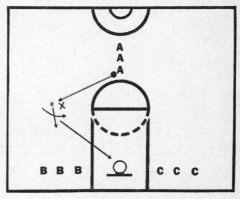

Diagram 15-5

there is no backcut. B, however, receives the pass, reverse-pivots and drives to the basket. C rebounds and rotates counterclockwise. The catch and the pivot by B are as important as the drive in this move. B catches the ball in the air so that he alights on both feet. He can then use either foot for a pivot foot to make the quick drop-step past his man and drive to the basket. The drop-step is a step back toward the basket with the foot opposite the defensive pressure, as shown in Diagram 15-5. A variation of this move needs to be shown and practiced in anticipation of the possibility that the defense might play directly behind B so that he can't use the drop-step. B now reverse-pivots on either foot rather than using a front pivot. A front pivot would carry B into the defense while the reverse pivot takes him away as shown in Diagram 15-6. Following the reverse pivot, B assumes the triple-threat position for the one-on-one drive to the basket.

This drill should be practiced from both sides. Beginning with the second week of practice, I like to add the fourth line to play defense on B. Now B must learn to read his defensive man and react. Also, it is good that B has real defense against him during his drive to the basket. He must learn when and when not to drive. I encourage the players at the B position in this drill to try the drive but also to be prepared to take the quick jump shot if the defense sags. This drill serves a dual purpose in that it simultaneously gives players defensive and offensive work.

This concludes the illustration of the two-man shooting drills.

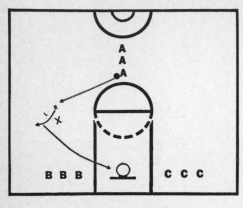 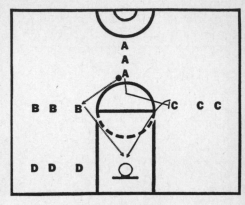

Diagram 15-6   **Diagram 15-7**

Three-Man Shooting Drills

The three-man shooting drills begin with Diagram 15-7 where A passes to B, either from the dribble or from a stationary position. A then goes to the opposite side of the floor to screen for C, using a two-footed jump-screen. A and C coordinate their efforts so that the necessary timing discussed in Chapter 13 is achieved. C breaks over the top of the screen for the crossover lay-up. D rebounds and follows his pass clockwise to line B.

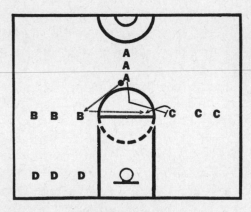

Diagram 15-8

This drill can be varied to practice the perimeter jump shot off the screen, as seen in Diagram 15-8.

Diagram 15-9 illustrates the drill used to simulate the screening action against a switching defense. Player A lands in his two-footed jump-screen and immediately reverse-pivots off his baseline foot for the pass from B. It is convenient for this drill if the rebounder, D, passes to line C and then takes a position there. C goes to line A, A goes to line B and B goes to line D.

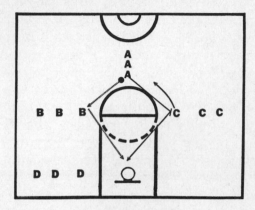

Diagram 15-9

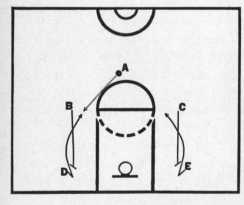

Diagram 15-10

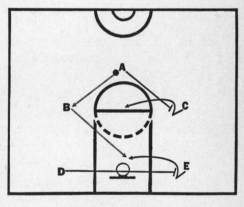

Diagram 15-11

Drills useful for teaching the low-post passing game and for practicing the shots from the offensive formation can be seen in Diagrams 15-10 and 15-11. Diagram 15-10 shows B and C screening down for D and E, who coordinate their feints to the inside with the screens by B and C. The screens are two-footed jump-screens. D and E break to the ball and A can pass to either as soon as they clear the screens. In this case, A passes to D who begins to square to the basket before he gets the ball. By the time D has caught the ball and brought it to a shooting position, he should be facing the basket. This procedure helps guarantee that he will be able to get the shot away—a valuable technique for the passing game where guards are exchanging positions with forwards. Note that B and C roll after their screens. A variation of this drill would be to spend a session passing to the screeners, B and C, on their roll. This drill can be varied even more by having them roll to the outside and receive the pass for a jump shot. This latter move is necessary against switching sagging defenses.

A very beneficial variation of this drill is to place defensive men on D and E. Player A must now find the open man, whether he is the cutter or the roller. The screeners, B and C, must be coached to roll either inside or outside depending on what the defense does. This is done by reverse-pivoting on the foot that is on the side that the defense attempts to fight past. The reverse pivot blocks the defense for an additional second, freeing the teammate cutting to the ball. It also keeps the defense on the back of the screener, giving him an open path to the ball. I like to have the team split into two groups for this drill, one at each end of the gym. I also like to have the players rotate after each attempt to familiarize them with each of the positions.

Diagram 15-11 illustrates the cross screens. Here A passes to one of the wings, B, and goes opposite to screen for C. D, who is now on the ballside, goes opposite to screen for E. C and E coordinate their cuts with the screens by B and D. B can pass to either. If he passes to C, C is to jump shoot. If he passes to E, E can jump shoot, hook or lay the ball up. Again, it is wise to have the players rotate after each execution so that they can operate from each of the positions.

One final comment before leaving the shooting drills and moving on to discuss the passing drills is that while they are called shooting drills, they teach other fundamentals at the same time: passing, pivoting, position, screening and rolling. It is both timesaving and efficient to utilize multiple purpose drills.

Passing Drills

While noting that all of the coaching drills for the passing game emphasize passing, two specialized passing drills are included here because they simulate realistic passing situations found in the actual offense.

The first of these drills is found in Diagram 15-12. The players are divided into four lines and placed in the four corners of the front court, slightly wider than the key area. The first player in line A initiates the offense by passing to line B and then going away to screen for the first player in line C. A uses the two-footed jump-screen and rolls to the inside, using his inside foot as his pivot foot. It is important that C coordinate his cut off A's screen by stepping to the inside and then making his cut at the exact instant that A leaves the floor to begin his jump. Meanwhile, B passes to D and goes away to screen for the player who is now at the front of line A. Next, D passes to C and goes to screen for B and so on. This is a fast-moving drill that players like to run, and they should run it at full speed. It teaches the pass-and-screen-away concept which is the essence of the passing game, and it teaches good screening technique. Various passes can be substituted for practice: the overhead pass, the bounce pass, the chest pass, or the baseball pass. The drill can and should be run in both clockwise and counterclockwise directions.

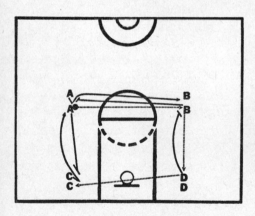

Diagram 15-12

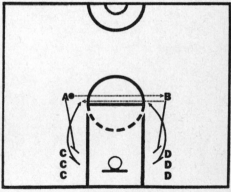

Diagram 15-13

The second passing drill, found in Diagram 15-13, uses two players in the guard positions and the remainder of the squad divided into two lines and placed at the baseline on either side of the key. The drill is initiated by A passing to the other guard, B, and going to the baseline to screen on the imaginary defensive player there. The first player in that line coordinates his cut off the screen with A's jump-screen and takes a return pass from B, who goes to screen for the player at the front of the line at the baseline. The passes all go from guard to guard in this drill, and there is no cross-screening. The players breaking out to receive the ball should be coached to gather the pass in as they are in the act of turning to a triple-threat position facing the basket.

I like to use this drill to teach and evaluate screening technique throughout the year. I do this by placing a defensive player on the baseline players, as shown in Diagram 15-14, or on the baseline players and the guard as well, as seen in Diagram 15-15. By having the guards either switch on defense or fight through the screens, I can get offensive practice for reading defensive reaction as well as teaching proper technique.

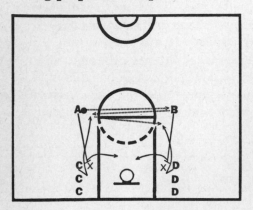

Diagram 15-14

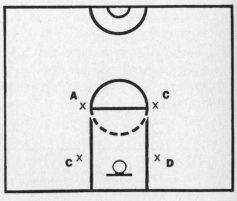

Diagram 15-15

One coaching reminder is that the cuts and screens should be executed at full speed but still under control, to prevent lazy defensive play. Also, I like to use these drills early in the season to introduce proper screening technique and proper cutting off the screen.

Some Thoughts on the Use of the Passing Drills

When I am coaching the low-post passing game, I use the drills that I have just illustrated in preparation for the passing game itself. When I am satisfied that the players have mastered the desired fundamentals implicit in these drills, I demonstrate the low-post passing game and have the players run it without defensive interference for several practices until I feel they are comfortable with it. I do not abandon these drills at this point, however. I try to use four of them each night and insist on concentration and execution. Short series of repetition over a long period of time is the best method for teaching this and other offenses.

Once the players are comfortable with the offense, I face them with actual defensive pressure. I do not allow the defense to switch for a while. I want to encourage good passing, good screening and good rolling technique. I also want to cultivate the ability to find the open man. I do not want any player to stand for more than one second; they must apply the rules and move.

When the players exhibit the ability to do these things, the defense is allowed to switch. Now, I look for the one-on-one drive by the wings or for the immediate roll to the basket by all screeners to take advantage of the switches, as described in Chapter 13.

I do have other drills that I introduce for fun and variety later in the season. These are discussed in the final section of this chapter.

When I am teaching the high-post passing game, I use all of the shooting and passing drills previously illustrated. In addition, I spend concentrated practice time with both the post and outside players separately. This concentrated practice is done by separating the posts to work at one end of the gym from the outside players who work at the other end.

The outside players drill by playing three-on-three from the formation that they will be using in the offense. As seen in Diagram 15-16, they must pass and screen away. They may not come above the foul line extended to get the ball. They can drive but not dribble for the sake of dribbling. A manager officiates and keeps score. He also enforces the one-second-then-move rule. Violation of any of these rules is penalized by loss of the ball.

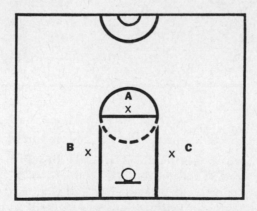

Diagram 15-16

For variety they play three-on-three with the manager being a stationary post player. The ball must be passed to the post a predetermined number of times before they can shoot. The manager can't shoot or play defense and he is still the referee.

Full court one-on-one is a useful drill for the outside players. It is a good conditioner and a good defensive drill.

Drills for the Posts

While the outside men are playing three-on-three, the posts drill for their specialized inside play. I like to begin their specialization by teaching them to interchange. The vertical interchange drill is shown in Diagram 15-17. The posts take their positions, one high and one low, on opposite sides of the key. The ball is passed slowly out front by the managers or by you and one manager who are at simulated guard positions. To begin, the ball is on the same side of the key as the high post for one second and then passed to the other side. Simultaneously, the high post breaks low as the low post breaks high on the ball side. Then the ball is passed back to the point of origin and the posts interchange again.

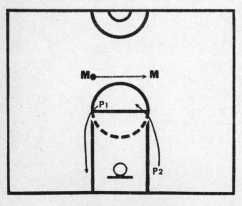 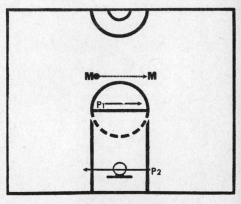

Diagram 15-17   **Diagram 15-18**

Diagram 15-18 illustrates the horizontal interchange. The ball is again passed back and forth out front. The high post then stays parallel with the ball while the low post goes opposite.

The purpose of both these drills is to teach the posts to work together by reading both the position of the ball and each other. For variety, the ball may be passed occasionally to either of the posts at which point the other post is to break immediately to the basket for a lay-up.

The posts are also coached to work for position and to react to all overplays. Working from the high post, as in Diagram 15-19, one post plays defense on the other by overplaying slightly. The offensive player receives the pass from the coach at the point, drop-steps with the foot farthest from the defense and drives to the basket. This is practiced by all posts and by overplaying from either side. If the defense plays so high that the direct pass to the post from out front is denied, the post breaks to the basket for the lob pass.

Diagrams 15-20 and 15-21 show the same drill from the low-post position with the defense placed high and low respectively. The technique is the same and should be practiced from both sides of the key.

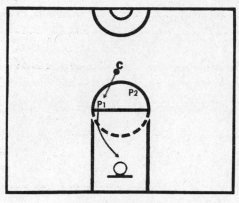

Diagram 15-19

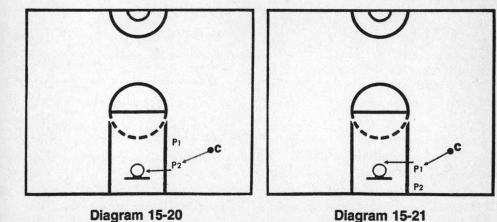

Diagram 15-20   **Diagram 15-21**

This concludes the specialized drills for the high post passing game. At this point, I include some general drills for fun and variety.

General Drills

1. The ball must be passed for a specified number of times (eg. 3, 4, 5, etc.) before a shot can be taken from the passing game offense.

2. While running the passing game, only lay-ups may be taken. No other shot is allowed. (Usually this works best if the defense isn't allowed to switch.)

3. No dribbles and no drives are allowed while running the passing game in this drill. No shots may be taken either. The object is to see how many passes can be completed before a loss of the ball occurs. Records should be kept and posted, and players should be encouraged to try to better them.

4. In the high-post passing game, the ball must be penetrated to the high post by passing and then returned to the perimeter at least three times before the offense is allowed to take a shot.

These drills all emphasize movement and passing. Remember that whether this offense is called "passing game" or "motion offense," patience screening, passing and movement are vital to success. Tell your players that. Believe it yourself. Also, remember that poor teams will succumb to two or three passes, while the good teams can withstand six or more passes before yielding a scoring opportunity for the offense. If there is truth to the old saw, "You play like you practice," then you must practice patience to beat the good teams.

16

Coaching the Keep-Away Game: Passing Game for Zones

Teams that execute the passing game well are certain to face zone defenses. Zones will be employed by teams who do not have the player talent to play good defense beyond the second pass of the passing game. Other teams will sag towards the middle on defense and switch on all screens by sloughing off their men. Both of these defenses are willing to give up the outside shot. They do not want to let the passing game get its characteristically good percentage shot.

Coaches of teams using the passing game are faced at this point with poor percentage basketball. By shooting from the outside, shooting percentages are sure to go down, and rebounding missed attempts will be difficult against the clogged middle. A defense may sag to the point where penetration by the offense is nearly impossible. Since the offense cannot penetrate the defense, they must shoot over the defense or employ some other strategy. Whatever course of action is taken, it should depend on the coach's philosophy and should have been prepared for.

I prefer to use the keep-away game against these "air-tight" zones and against sloughing, sagging man-to-man defenses. I like to dictate my style of play to the defense. I want my teams to play smart basketball and keep the percentages of the game in their favor. I feel that the defensive team that has just switched from man-to-man defense to zone defense has admitted that it can not play the freewheeling high-scoring game. They desire to change the tempo and the style of play that will swing the percentages of the game to their favor. I also feel that if the offense fails to adjust its game plan and allows the percentages of the game to remain with the defense, then the offense is playing to lose. The keep-away game is our answer to sagging man-to-man and zone defenses.

Purposes of the Keep-Away Game

Most teams will switch from man-to-man to zone when they are behind. If they are ahead they hesitate to change the tempo of the game or make an adjustment that could change the outcome. The obvious exceptions to this occur if the defensive team is ahead late in the ball game and they try to protect a lead by trying to make the offense shoot long shots or, if they switch to a zone when the score is tied, they may be trying to gain an advantage while the offense attempts to adjust. For discussion purposes here, I will assume that neither of these two situations is the case.

The keep-away game can only be used when the score is tied or when the team in control of the basketball is ahead since the success of the keep-away offense depends on the "lack of sufficient action" rule. This rule is discussed in detail later. It is enough for the present to say that the keep-away uses the rule when they are ahead or when the score is tied, when the other team is in a zone defense and for the following purposes:

1. To spread the defense so that it can be penetrated.
2. To control the ball with minimal risk until a good percentage shot can be taken.
3. To provide an organized method of attacking zones.
4. To consume time from the clock late in the game.
5. To protect or increase your lead.
6. To use an offense that affords possibilities of three-point plays late in the game.
7. To isolate your better ball players for one-on-one play.

Advantages and Disadvantages

Before deciding to use the keep-away game, you should look closely at the advantages and disadvantages to see if it is consistent with your philosophy. The advantages of the keep-away game are:

1. The keep-away game allows the offense to continue to play man-to-man.
2. The keep-away cuts down on the risk of poor percentage shots over the top of zone defenses.
3. It dicates the style of play to the defense since the defense must play at least partial man-to-man.
4. The keep-away game is flexible; it can be used as a stall, a delay game or a scoring offense.
5. It is easy to teach.
6. It uses a formation similar to the low-post passing game, which makes it easier for players to learn if they use the low-post passing game.
7. The keep-away game can be used against all defenses.
8. It is an offense that allows you to protect players who are in foul trouble late in the game.

The disadvantages of the keep-away game are as follows:

1. By using the keep-away game you will slow the tempo of the game. You will have to determine whether this is bad or good.
2. It is not always popular with crowds since it does slow the tempo of the game.
3. The keep-away game doesn't work at all when you are behind unless the defense is pressuring the ball.

Factors to Consider Concerning the Rule Book

Because the keep-away game tries to draw the defense away from the basket, the offense begins with the ball near mid-court. In fact, much of the offensive play of the keep-away game is in or near the mid-court area. Consequently, there are some considerations regarding play in the mid-court area.

The Lack of Sufficient Action Rule

The keep-away game is based on the "lack of sufficient action" rule as set forth in Rule 10, section 2 (c) of the National Federation of State High School Associations edition of the rules. In its "Comments on the Rules," the Federation says, "lack of sufficient action occurs when the team responsible for action: 1. Permits the ball to remain in its mid-court for 10 seconds, during which time there is no opposing action in this area; or 2. Does not continuously and aggressively attempt to gain control of the ball within 10 seconds while the ball is in the mid-court of the opponents."

Since this discussion assumes that the team with the ball is ahead, then the lack of sufficient action rule dictates that the defensive team must "continuously and aggressively attempt to gain control of the ball" when it is in the mid-court for a period of five seconds. If the score is tied, then the defense must supply sufficient action.

Therefore, when a team is on offense when the score is tied or while they are ahead and their opponents are in a sagging zone near the basket to prevent the high-percentage shot, then the keep-away game can be used to exploit the lack of sufficient action rule to draw the defense away from the basket.

When properly enforced, the lack of sufficient action rule carries the penalty of a technical foul for each infraction. This, of course, works to the advantage of the offensive team since they get a free throw plus possession of the ball at mid-court. Repeated refusal by the defense to use sufficient action in an attempt to secure possession of the ball should lead to forfeiture of the game.

The Held-Ball Rule

Another rule that is a factor when employing the keep-away game is the held-ball rule, Rule 4, section 15 (c) which says, "a held ball occurs when a closely guarded player, in his or her mid-court, dribbles or combines dribbling and holding the ball for 5 seconds." This rule obviously requires that a team, even though ahead in terms of score, must produce action of its own if closely guarded by the defense. In commenting on the rules, the Federation explains that the purpose of the rule is "to discourage 'freezing' or 'keep-away' tactics, during which there is little or no attempt to score." This presents no problem to a team using the keep-away game. Despite its name, the purpose of the keep-away offense is to score, but it prefers to be selective in its choice of shots.

The held ball rule is mentioned here since the keep-away offense begins in the mid-court area and since players in the offense must be made aware of the rule.

Offensive players must know that "closely guarded" will depend on referees' judgment. They should know that many referees will use the distance of six feet as a rule of thumb, so long as the guard has assumed a legal guarding position.

The players must also realize that "combining holding and dribbling" means that the five-second time limit begins when holding the ball while being closely guarded and continues through a subsequent dribble.

Players must further understand a principle contained in the "Comments on the Rules" that says, "If a player, who is closely guarding an opponent, switches his or her assignment with a teammate without breaking the continuity of the closely guarding status, the count shall continue uninterrupted." This means that an offensive player with the ball may elude his guard, but not have eluded his closely guarded status because of an effective switch by the defense.

Thus, this action of the held ball rule means that "closely guarding" by the defense, whether by one guard on the player with the ball or by more than one player executing cooperative and continuous action on the ball, forces the offense to stop the existing five-second count by passing, dribbling out of the mid-court area designated by the hash marks on either sideline or by eluding the defense. The keep-away offense uses the "closely guarded" status to signal the intiation of the offense. Since the rule dictates that the ball must be moved when the player holding it is closely guarded, this is a good and logical method of beginning.

Before discussing the offensive movement further, let's look at the basic formation of the offense.

Basic Formation and Personnel Placement

Diagram 16-1 illustrates the basic formation of the keep-away game against a very tight 2-1-2 zone defense. Consistent with our previous discussions regarding the use of the keep-away game, it can now be assumed that the offense is ahead, or at the very least the score is tied. The defense wishes to maintain a very tight formation, even to the point of inviting the outside shot.

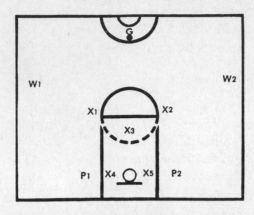

Diagram 16-1

The point guard holds the ball near the division line in his mid-court area. It is important that he be far enough away from the division line so that if he moves a leg backward, as in a pivot move, he would not violate the "over-and-back" rule as set forth in Rule 9, section 9.

The point guard, G, should not attempt to pass the ball or waste his dribble at this juncture. He should hold the ball and wait for the defensive team to exert sufficient action.

Notice the positions taken by the wings, W1 and W2. They are very wide, perhaps only a step-and-a-half from the sidelines. They are outside the mid-court area designated by the hash marks. The positioning of the wings is very important. If they are out of the mid-court area, then any pass to them breaks the five-second count. By being in a triangular configuration with the point guard, they maintain good passing angles and lanes from the point. If the wings were placed parallel with the point, there would be no passing angle, and the defensive players guarding the wings would have good opportunity to steal any pass to that area. Also, with all three players very close to the division line, a bad pass could result in an accidental over-and-back violation.

The wings should be good drivers to execute this offense properly. They add real punch to the offense if they are good jump shooters from a distance of eight to ten feet.

The post players, P1 and P2, are placed one step outside of the free-throw lane so that they don't accidentally step into the lane and violate the three-second rule. The posts need to be rugged rebounders and understand the fundamental principles of post play and post position. They add much to the offense if they can consistently score on eight-foot jumpers from the baseline.

The Basic Offense and Options

Diagram 16-2 essentially captures the entire offense of the keep-away game. When one of the defensive guards, in this case X1, moves out on the ball to force sufficient action, G simply passes the ball to the wing man on the side from which the defensive pressure came. Here G passes to W1.

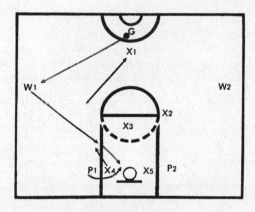

Diagram 16-2

Once W1 has the ball, he looks to see what X3, the defensive middle man is doing. W1 hopes to be able to find an opening between X3 and X4 large enough to get through without getting double-teamed. W1 thereby hopes to make X4 leave P1's area and stop the dribble penetration. W1 would then pass to P1 for the lay-up or for the high-percentage jump shot.

It may be that W1 can't penetrate on his first attempt and will simply hold the ball until X1 comes to cover him, then passing it back out to G. Or, he may have started to drive and then dribbled back out to his wing position. Or, he may have penetrated as in Diagram 16-2 far enough to take the good, open, eight-foot jump shot.

It is important that the offense be very patient while running the keep-away game. The players must remember that they are not behind on the scoreboard, that they want to add to their score and increase their lead at the same time.

Coaching Hints for the Keep-Away Game

Like all offenses, the keep-away game relies on many little things to be successful. You will want to stress these things in practice.

The first of these hints is that the driving wing wants to beat the middle man and make the nearest baseline man pick him up. At the same time, both baseline offensive men anticipate that this will happen and try to secure an open path to the ball or rebound position. Usually the post on the ball side will move to the basket.

All players should be aware of the defensive player nearest them. If the defensive player in their area fails to watch them closely, they should break to the basket. If they do not get the ball immediately, they should resume their normal positions.

This back-door sneak is particularly successful when done by one of the wings when the other wing has the ball, as in Diagram 16-3. G has passed the ball to W1 at the wing. X1 stays with G in man-to-man coverage, and X3 vacates the middle to pressure the ball and W1. X2 now fills the middle to cover the area vacated by X3. This frees W2 for the cut to the basket and the resulting pass from W1.

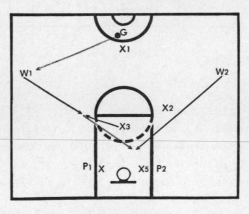

Diagram 16-3

Finally, since this offense isolates the player with the ball, quite often near the basket, players need to be coached to make a real attempt to score when they get within six to eight feet from the basket. Not only does this make the offense a threat, but it also results in many three-point plays.

Cycling the Keep-Away Game for Continuity

The continuity for the keep-away game is best achieved by the simple rule of thumb that requires floor balance by maintaining basic positions or by filling a vacated position.

The posts maintain their basic positions, moving, of course, to get open. They can exchange positions with each other, and they can post up whenever a player cuts through their area.

The outside players try to maintain the basic formations by keeping their positions or by filling vacated ones. This filling of vacated positions is accomplished by one of four maneuvers.

The first of these uses the give-and-go move, as seen in Diagram 16-4. Any player can execute a give-and-go, and the give-and-go can be a delayed move. In Diagram 16-4, for instance, G has passed to W1. W1 may not choose to drive and may not be able to pass back to G. In this case, G breaks to the basket. If he is not open he has, at least, vacated a position for W2 to break into to receive the ball.

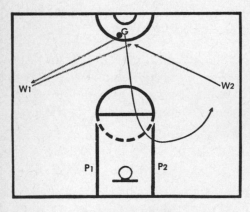

Diagram 16-4

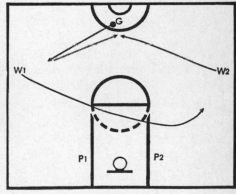

Diagram 16-5

The second maneuver to maintain floor balance is seen in Diagram 16-5. This move has been called the dribble-chase, and I like the name because it describes the action. G dribbles the ball at W1 (perhaps because he was unable to pass to him), and chases W1 toward the basket and out the other side of the key. W2 rotates to the point for the return pass if G didn't choose to hit P1 who posted when W1 cut off him and didn't even hit W1 on his cut.

The third move is similar to the dribble-chase, and it is seen in Diagram 16-6. Here G (or any outside player for that matter) begins a drive, aborts it and comes out of the key. In Diagram 16-6, he comes out on W2's side of the floor and chases him to the vacant point position.

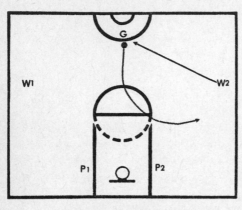 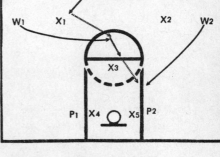

Diagram 16-6   **Diagram 16-7**

The last of these maneuvers is referred to as a circle-out. In Diagram 16-7 we see that G drives hard at X1 instead of at W1. X1 is compelled to move out to guard G while W1 moves behind X1 for the pass. W1 now drives hard at X2 allowing W2 to cut behind him for the drop-pass. W2 then drives hard at X3, allowing G to penetrate the middle if G picks up W2. If either X4 or X5 move to help, then P1 or P2 will be open next to the basket.

Using the Keep-Away Game Against Man-to-Man

The keep-away game can be used as a regular offense against the man-to-man defense, but it really becomes another offense when that happens.

What this section of this chapter is concerned with is how the keep-away game should respond to a sudden and immediate switch by the defense from zone to man-to-man.

There are two basic reactions to such defensive pressure, and the one you choose should depend on the kind of regular man-to-man offense you employ for the sake of offensive coherence and simplicity.

Usually, a move by the defense to pick up man-to-man will come from a zone that has already matched up initial alignment. For instance, in Diagram 16-8, the defense's 1-2-2 zone is a good match-up for the keep-away basic set. Once the defense moves out to pick up man-to-man, a good response is to break a post high, hit him from the point and then cut past him to the basket, as in Diagram 16-9.

As you have probably recognized, Diagram 16-9 is, in essence, the high-post passing game. Once this move has been made, the offense should continue in the high-post passing game as long as the defense stays man-to-man.

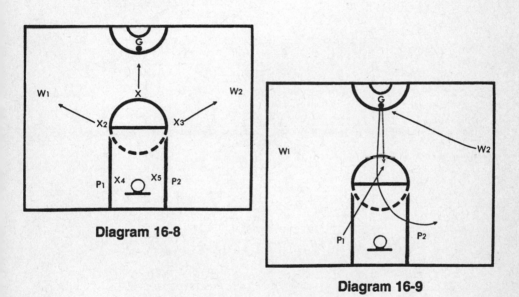

Diagram 16-8

Diagram 16-9

It should be noted here that if your basic offense is the 1-4, then you should break both posts high to begin, as in Diagram 16-10. If you are using the shuffle offense, break one post opposite and break the wing on that side over the top of that post to initiate the offense. This is seen in Diagram 16-11. If the triple stack is used, you will notice that Diagram 16-9 is virtually the same as the triple stack trap play.

Finally, if you are using the low-post passing game, you will want to respond similarly to the move shown in Diagram 16-12. The point guard holds the ball while the wings break low to screen for the posts, and the low-post passing game, as described in Chapter 13, is underway.

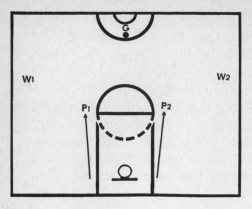

Diagram 16-10

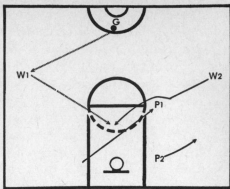

Diagram 16-11

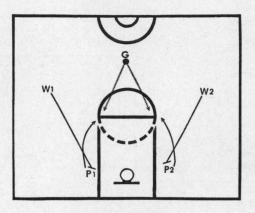

Diagram 16-12

A Parting Word

One final note at this point would be that, as promised at the outset, all of the offenses in this book can be used separately or blended to your own choosing. Hopefully, these last pages illustrate that point again. Here, we have blended the keep-away offense with each of the offenses discussed in this book. I know that I have not had space to cover all the combinations possible. I have not even covered all the combinations that I have used in my coaching system. Perhaps the only real limits to the possibilities for combining the offenses presented would be one's imagination and one's philosophy.

Index